LIVERP[O]
IRISH
CONNECTION
BY MICHAEL KELLY

Ellen Tate

James Muspratt

Agnes Jones

Percy French

Michael James Whitty

Published by
AJH Publishing
54 Brows Lane
Formby
L37 4ED

Printed by
Ribcar
56 Lower Breck Road
Tuebrook, Liverpool
L6 4BZ

ISBN 0-9554854-0-1
ISBN 978-0-9554854-0-4

Dedication

This book is respectfully dedicated to my grandparents
Maurice Patrick and Mary Ann Kelly
and
James and Mary Doyle

To my parents
Michael and Margaret

To my brother Peter
who sadly died in 2002

Other works by Michael Kelly

Merseyside Tales
A collection of short stories

The Life and Times of Kitty Wilkinson
A most remarkable woman, born in County Derry, Ireland, but
living most of her remarkable life caring and working for the poor in Liverpool.
This is a biography not to missed by any serious student of civic history.

Contents

Acknowledgements

Many of the people I wish to thank, for encouraging and helping me to continue and finish this project, were people outside, what might be called the Irish community. However they are people who have a love and respect for Liverpool and the surrounding area and they acknowledge the part the Irish have played in the development of Liverpool.

I wish to thank Rosemary Morris for editing this work and for her valuable advice and great patience. My thanks also to Co. Donegal sisters, Mary Devlin and Margaret McGrath, for their support and for introducing me to Buncrana and Derry Libraries. Jane Walsh for her encouragement and critical analysis of my work over the years and a friendship I could always count on. Eileen Robinson, the Liverpool Connection bookshop, is not only an owner but a source of inspiration and encouragement to any would-be writer. My thanks to Margaret Graham, a thorough daughter of Scotland for all her help and advice, and Tom Morley, for publishing my early work.

My thanks to Josie McCann, for helping to correct my work and Marie McQuade, for her support, allowing me to delve into her research work on family history. Thanks also to David Charters, journalist and columnist with the 'Liverpool Daily Post' for his wonderful support in highlighting my work in his newspaper and also for permission to use a photo of Michael James Whitty. Tony Baker, of the Friends of Anfield Cemetery for his support in directing me to the family graves of Michael James Whitty, Alderman Richard Shiel and Christopher Corbally. A special thanks to Ron Formby, editor of the Scottie Press, community newspaper for his support in promoting my work and for being the best community worker I know.

My thanks to Cheniston K Roland, violin and music historian for introducing me to the Liverpool Athenaeum and allowing me full use of its beautiful library whose staff have been a tremendous help. I wish to express my gratitude to the staff of Liverpool Central Library, Crosby Library Sefton, Merseyside, and the staff of The National Library of Ireland, Dublin who supplied me with a five year reader's card, which I treasure. The 'Irish Post' for publishing my article on Michael James Whitty and Kitty Wilkinson, 'The Derry Journal' and 'The Inish Times', for mentioning that I was writing a book on the Liverpool Irish. I am indebted to BBC Radio Merseyside and presenters, Roger Phillips, Roger Lyons, Lynda McDermott and Station Manager, Mick Ord, for allowing me to speak about my work.

I am indebted to artist Anthony Brown, art director of 'Emso Illustration Fine Art Design' for supporting me. My thanks to 'Ireland's Own' a family magazine of the highest standard and to editors, Margaret Galvin, Phil Murphy and Sean Nolan, for their continuous encouragement. It was this gem of a magazine that first brought to public notice my work on the Liverpool Irish.

My thanks to John Towell for the waterfront illustration on the front cover and Phil Finegan of Ribcar for his help and understanding.

Introduction

Although growing up in Liverpool, I learned almost nothing of the Liverpool Irish during my schooldays, but from an early age I was exposed to a kind of music that told stories of a mystical land across the Irish Sea. The songs conveyed sadness and happiness and conjured up glimpses of a land of open spaces and rivers that ran free. There were people who spoke with a dialect that sounded like my grandparents and without knowing it then, its essence was an unseen umbilical cord. It was only when I reached my teens and started to move away from my home and community that I realised the phraseology used by others was different to what I had grown up with. My grandparents had long gone and so had many of the other senior members of that community but their mannerisms and use of language was locked in my mind.

It was during this journey through life that I heard the words 'poverty' and 'ghetto' in connection with the Liverpool Irish and it took me some years to understand the use of those terms. After all I was on a journey through life and had no time to look back at the past, but somehow the past catches up with one. It was then that I started to look at the early Irish settlers into Liverpool. It was without difficulty that my mind settled on the late eighteenth and nineteenth centuries to study the Liverpool Irish. This was a time of great hunger and mass poverty and Liverpool, like a mother giving birth, suffered pain and discomfort and saw only the strongest of her brood growing up and helping to build a great seaport.

Liverpool was made up from a number of different nationalities who contributed to the development of the town but it was the Irish, my own clansmen, who took my attention. Most of them were never ashamed to say they had lived in poverty although not all of them did and it was this more affluent section of the Irish community, the more able, that impressed me most.

I make no excuses for using a number of full quotes from the newspapers of the nineteenth century to describe many of the people portrayed in the book. The use of the English language, during that period, help to take the reader back to an age, long gone, when the beauty of the language more accurately reflected the events of the nineteenth century

For many centuries the Irish have been crossing the Irish Sea to settle in places like Liverpool. As far back as 1378, there were Irish burgesses in Liverpool. Britain had created the industrial revolution and Liverpool at that period was an expanding seaport and needed people.

They came from everywhere in Britain and as Ireland was part of the United Kingdom during the nineteenth century its people had every right to settle in Liverpool along with the Welsh and the Scots. They also joined the many regiments of a fellow Irishman, the Duke of Wellington.

There had always been visiting merchants engaged in the Irish trade, but not until the late eighteenth-century was there much of an Irish colony in the town. John Denvir could never have envisaged in 1892, that the time would come when in Liverpool, the Irish would through their endeavours occupy every field in commerce, the professions, science and the theatre. The growth of the Irish in the town can be traced by the increase of Irish names in the town directories first published in 1766.

An important major influx to Liverpool was that which followed the 1798 rebellion in Ireland. This growth in the Irish population resulted in the Irish playing an increasing large roll in the economic political and religious life of the city. The increase in Roman Catholics can be seen in the number of churches built and the increasing number of Catholic Church records, especially after the opening of St. Patrick's, St. Nicolas, Copperas Hill and St Anthony's, by the 1820s, testify to the relatively rapid influx. In 1841 about 20% of the total Irish in England and Wales were to be found in the Liverpool area. The Welsh and the Scots also arrived and this Celtic mix, created a town like no other in England. Paul Cohen-Portheim, describes the various traits of the Celts, in his book, 'England The Unknown Isle':

> But the most genuine Celts are, after all, the Irish, doubtless in consequence of their insular position. The Irishman is the most mystical, the most fanatical, and the most ruled by his instincts and perhaps the most talented of the lot, and his country is the land of legend and poetry. Ireland has given Great Britain many of her greatest poets and writers, but every Irishman has something of the poet, or at least of the visionary, in him.

The people who had access to a good education before leaving Ireland helped to create the fabric of the great seaport of Liverpool. They used their knowledge in the field of medicine, law, and commerce both at national and local level. Irish men and women have created many of Liverpool's finest institutions.

Commenting on the terrible insanitary conditions in Liverpool, John Denvir in his book 'The Irish in Britain' published in 1892, wrote:

> There has been, however, a vast change for the better in the surroundings of our people, and, indeed in every other way, so that there is no town in the country in which we have made greater progress than in Liverpool. Irishmen are gradually emerging from the ranks of the unskilled labour and becoming more numerous among the artisans, shopkeepers, merchants and the professional classes. Among the latter they have most distinctly made their mark. Among Irish lawyers of the highest reputation, Sir Charles Russell may be said to have graduated on this circuit.
>
> The Irish doctors of Liverpool are numerous, and the first in their profession. The Irish of Liverpool frequently show a remarkable attitude for dealing, which goes to show that, under the fostering care of a

native government, ours would develop into a great commercial people. So by degrees they got into higher circles of the commercial world, and of these there are to be seen, among the merchant princes on 'Change' men who either themselves or whose fathers before them commenced life in Liverpool as corn or cotton porters, or even in some humbler or more precarious occupations.

The Irish names of Liverpool people can still be seen in almost every institution, and on the front of many businesses throughout Merseyside. The decision to build Liverpool's world famous Royal Liver Building, erected in 1911 on Liverpool's historic waterfront, was taken in a Dublin office. To quote John Denvir once again in his praise for the Liverpool Irish and their adopted town:

> Liverpool contains next to London, the largest population of any town in Great Britain. They are not scattered about in handfuls, as you find them in the metropolis, but massed together in great numbers. Among them the late A. M. Sullivan used to say he felt as if he were 'not out of Ireland at all, but on a piece of the old sod itself'. Of the Irishmen holding positions in the diocese the following are in the borough of Liverpool itself, two magistrates, nine town councillors, four Poor-Law Guardians and four members of the School Board.
> Liverpool is the only place in Great Britain able to return a Nationalist to Parliament for one of its seats against all comers. As this is the only constituency in Great Britain in our hands, Mr T. P. O'Connor may be said to represent not merely the Scotland Division, nor Liverpool, but the whole of England, Scotland and Wales. Liverpool has furnished no less then eight members of the Irish Parliamentary Party since its formation. It is not without some justification that some consider it the Irish capital of England.

The descendents of Irish settlers into the town still fill many of the seats not only in the Council Chamber but among the professional and business community.

What began as a slow flowing stream in the mid-eighteen-hundreds soon flowed faster and turned into a rushing torrent as the dark clouds of famine and poverty took a hold on the poorest people in Ireland. Liverpool had very little to offer those who arrived during the famine years, except the chance of a new life if they were prepared to work and accept the poverty of a newly expanding seaport.

They were prepared to take on any form of hard and heavy work that needed a strong frame and a stout heart. In the 1860s a metal bucket used as a drinking vessel to quench the thirst of a shire horse was of more value, than the life of a man working on the docks. A hundred years latter very little had changed, a man injured or killed could be replaced at the drop of a hat. It is doubtful if there was a British ship sailing out of the port of Liverpool that did not have Irishmen among its crew. During the first and second World Wars many paid with their lives.

1

Ellen Tate

Ellen Tate with her clay pipe

We are in a time where we expect people to live to a great age with the help of science, medication and hospital care. It is said that a characteristic of civilised nations is to venerate age, whether the individuals are 'fluent in rags, or flutter in brocade'. Mrs Ellen Tate was an example of longevity in the eighteen and nineteen centuries at a time when most poor people died before the age of twenty-five. Helen was born in 1713 in the parish of Killede, County Antrim. Her maiden name was Craig, but little is known of her family and early life. She was married to a schoolmaster, whose name was Tate and by whom she had four children. Two of them died at an early age and one became a mariner who sailed out of Liverpool and made the town his home after moving from County Antrim.

Ellen's husband had died when her children were still quite young, and she lived alone after her two remaining children had moved out to make a life for themselves. Life was very lonely for Ellen in her cottage in Killede, then her mariner son sent for her to move with him to a house he had acquired in the port of Liverpool. Ellen looked after the house and her son's affairs when he was away on a voyage. Her new life in the town soon started to blossom when she became a member of a local Church and made many new friends. Ellen became a part of the respectable society of the growing seaport and was often invited to afternoon tea by her Church-going friends.

Sadly her comfortable life fell apart with the death of her son who drowned at sea. When she reached sixty in 1773 (a great age in those days), not having any means of her own, she had to support herself by doing any job that came along in the market. There was no pension or state help in those days and Ellen was thankful for anything that came her way. After her job in the market failed due to lack of work she took to the streets with a basket on her head, containing religious tracks, laces and ribbons and other pieces of haberdashery.

Ellen continued to support herself in this fashion for more than thirty years, sooner than place herself at the mercy of the parish. Sadly the day came when she was too old to be walking the streets selling her goods with little profit in her occupation, so she was forced to apply to the parish as the last resort.

She was ninety-four at the time of entering the workhouse and soon became a favourite of the governor. Despite her great age she was in good health and had a highly retentive memory. She was allowed to visit the town centre when the mood took her and as the years passed by she became more of a curiosity with passers-by in the town centre who saw her smoking her clay pipe. Because of her advanced years she was allowed an extra allowance of tea, some ale and other comforts, supplied by the workhouse governor.

Strangers and the gentry who occasionally visited the workhouse, viewed her with veneration, and frequently gave her money. Ellen was still attending church at the time of her hundredth birthday, and eventually lived for another ten years, dying at the age of hundred and ten.

2

Sir William Brown

---He erected the Free Public Library and Derby Museum in Liverpool.

William Brown, born at Ballymena on 13th May, 1784, was the eldest son of Alexander and Grace Brown, both of Ballymena County Antrim Ireland. At twelve years of age he was placed under the care of the Rev. J. Bradley at Catterick, Yorkshire but in 1800 he returned to Ireland. Soon afterwards he sailed with his father and mother for the United States of America and they settled in Baltimore. His father continued in the linen trade in which he had been engaged in Ireland. In a few years the house at Baltimore became the firm of Alexander Brown & Sons, consisting of the father and his sons, William, John, George and James.

In 1809 William returned to the United Kingdom and established a branch of the firm in Liverpool and shortly afterwards the family abandoned the exclusive linen business and became general merchants. The transactions of the firm soon extended to further branches in New York, Philadelphia and Baltimore.

On 1 January 1810, William married Sarah, daughter of Andrew Gibson of Ballymena, and after the death of their father, George and John, who by this time had made ample fortunes, retired from the firm, leaving William and James, the youngest son, to continue. They now became bankers in the sense of conducting transmissions of money on public account between the two hemispheres and in this pursuit and the business of merchants, they acquired immense wealth.

William was the founder of the firm of Brown, Shipley, & Co., Liverpool and London merchants. In 1825 William took an active part in the agitation for the reform in the management of the Liverpool docks. He was elected an Alderman of Liverpool in 1831 and held that office until 1838. He was the unsuccessful Anti-Corn Law League candidate for South Lancashire in April 1844. He was, however, returned in 1846, and continued to represent South Lancashire until April 1859. Sarah his wife died on 5th March 1858. William Brown was created a Baronet on 24th Jan 1863 and in the same year served as Sheriff for the County of Lancashire. He did not, however, live long enough to enjoy his honours, as he died at Richmond Hill, Liverpool, on 3 March 1864.

The name of William Brown is probably best known for the magnificent gift, which he bestowed on his adopted town. He erected the Free Public Library and Derby Museum in Liverpool, which was opened on 8 October. 1860, at a cost to himself of £40,000, the corporation providing the site and furnishing of the building. William was honoured by Liverpool in having the site of the Library and Museum named after him. It is unlikely that there is another street like this in Britain. William Brown Street is almost entirely devoted to the arts. It is a magnet for visitors coming to the City of Liverpool because of its magnificent architecture on the north side of the street, which is overlooked by the splendor of St. George's Hall and St. John's Gardens on the south side. The Victorians gave Liverpool a grandeur that has never been equalled since.

3

Alderman Richard Sheil

---In a larger degree than most Irishmen, he has acquired the solid and practical character of Englishmen.

'The Porcupine'

Liverpool is a town of many parks and no other town in the U.K. has more, outside of London. One of these is Sheil Park, which runs along side of Sheil Road and most people passing through will not give a thought as to how it came by its name.

Sheil Park is named after Alderman Richard Henry Sheil, a very wealthy Liverpool merchant and Town Councillor. Richard was born in Tipperary in 1791. He was a cousin of Richard Lalor Sheil, dramatist and politician, and Sir Justin Sheil of Waterford. It is believed Richard was a purser in the navy for a short time. He later made his way to Haiti and the Gulf of Mexico where the Sheil family had many business interests.

It was while he was in Haiti that he met his future wife who was of French origin and Richard came to Liverpool in 1828 with her and carried on his business as a merchant. They had two sons and a daughter. However, their two sons died during their mature years but their daughter, married a Mr. Leonard, a cattle dealer. Richard still traded with Mexico and Cuba and his ability as a businessman soon found him respect with the local merchants. He was attracted to the Liberal Party because of his Catholic faith and he was a supporter of the 1832 Reform Act much to the disgust of those who used the council for their own personal gain.

He was elected to the new council in 1835 when the Municipal Reform Act was passed. As a Liberal he was the first and only Catholic in the chamber but soon gained respect from comrades and foes alike. Richard represented the people of Scotland Ward, a very Irish Catholic area of the town. Over the years other Irish men and women would also serve the Scotland Ward as well. The Right Hon. T. P. O'Connor was one of those who served as an Irish Nationalist Member of Parliament from 1885 to 1929.

The plight of the poor Catholic in Liverpool was always in the forefront of Richard's mind whenever he was in the council chamber but he also voiced his concern for all the poor people of the town. He fought for and won the right to have Catholic children attend Corporation Schools, which was long before universal education. His example in the council chamber helped increase trade between Liverpool and Ireland. 'The Porcupine' newspaper in an article 'Pen Portraits of Liverpool Town Councillors' wrote:

> Mr Sheil is an Irishman, and the only Roman Catholic in the council. He is of the same family as the late eminent barrister and statesman, the Right Honourable Richard Lalor Sheil, and Ireland has not a son who loves his country better than does the subject of our notice. He is ever found at the head of any movement, which, in his opinion, is calculated to promote her political or religious welfare, and his enthusiasm on such occasions shows with that heartiness and zeal he espouses the cause of Ireland. That Mr. Sheil looks upon his country as "the first

flower of the earth, the first gem of the sea," nobody can for a moment doubt and he spiritedly acts upon that conviction.

Mr. Sheil's complexion is dark, his eyes, which are black, are expressive, but they have a peculiar glare which it is difficult to characterise phraseologically and he has a look of abstractedness and fixedness which seems to defy penetration, and which one would rather expect to find in some Spanish monk of secluded and mystic life, than in a Liverpool merchant mixing freely with all classes of a busy community.

Mr. Sheil who has passed his sixtieth year, has become somewhat bald. He still, however, speaks with much animation, has a good clear voice, and like his countrymen, deals liberally in metaphor. He has, however, resided too long in England to be a mere flashy and flowery speaker. In a larger degree than most Irishmen he has acquired the solid and practical character of Englishmen. He takes a shrewd view of any subject under discussion, and his onslaught is always vigorous. The moment he utters a sentence, his pronunciation declares the place of his birth. A rich, mellifluous brogue poured out with volubility and with a swing of the arms and a jerking forward of the body, smack of Tipperary. Looking at the number of his countrymen located and shall we say naturalised, in Liverpool, and at the importance of the trade, Irish interests are but imperfectly represented in the council, although if the sister island is to be stinted to one champion and child, she could not easily select better than the gentleman of whom we speak. Mr. Sheil is no exception to the generality of his mercurial countrymen: he is made up of many ingredients, some of them of an opposite nature, yet all necessary to produce a genuine Hibernian. Mr. Sheil is an active member of the Health Committee, and would be serviceable as an administrator of the Dock Estate.

The value of reproducing pen portraits of the past gives the reader a chance to listen to the eloquent voices and use of the language in the council chamber in the nineteenth century. Once again we are reminded of the character of Richard Sheil and his value and love of his adopted town again in 'The Porcupine's', 'Pen Portraits of Liverpool Town Councillors' 9 September 1865.

On Wednesday last there was a rather sharp though very brief encounter between one of the oldest and one of the newest members of the council. The former was seen to laugh during, though not at, a speech of the latter. The new – we might almost say, the glossy member construed this into an offence, and said something to the effect that he hoped his remarks would prove worthy of the old member's consideration, though now he derided them. In an instant, the old gentleman was on his feet, he was sure, he said, that the speaker was labouring under some misconception: he had simply laughed at a remark made by the member next to him, and had no intention of interrupting the gentleman's "most eloquent address".

The incident is not much to relate: but those present witnessed it with great amusement and not a little pleasure. Though the old member was a Liberal and the new member a Tory, all sides felt that the latter had been guilty of a gratuitous impertinence, and all rejoiced that the generally esteemed subject of the affront had so amply and yet in so polished a manner resented it. The old member was Mr. Alderman Sheil. The half-ruffled yet wholly self-possessed manner in which he rebuffed the impertinence was a reminiscence of his best days, while the tribute of unusual and sympathetic hilarity betokened the popularity, which fitly rewards a long life spent in giving and taking hard knocks for principle's sake, with equal constancy and good humour.

Mr. Sheil is in the evening of his days, and though

he may yet continue for many years to grace as its centre, a private circle of rarely exampled harmony and geniality, his public life is about to close. He does well to drop into the apron of domesticity in the autumn bloom of his reputation, and not wither, as many do, out of knowledge and out of esteem on the tree of public affairs. While fully enjoying and appreciating the honours which have been formally and informally accorded him, he perceives, at the same time, that his vigour is lessening, and he retires from the exhausting race, not least he should be beaten, but lest the pace should prove too taxing for the remnants of his strength.

It is fit that we should take a retrospective view of the life of such a man, and when we do so we are struck by a sense of contrast between the earlier and the latter portion of Mr. Sheil's life. Mr. Sheil appears to have altered, because his character and the progress of his principles have altered the times and done away with the evils against which, for many years, he fiercely and fearlessly fought.

Mr. Sheil is a Liberal and a Catholic and both characters were, in his day, tabooed in Liverpool. But, in those characters, he stood boldly forth. He was a leader of men thirty years ago and what his generation struggled for our generation enjoys. He brought to public affairs the prestige of an unstained private character, and throughout his career he had the same valuable anchor.

Though the trade in which he was engaged encountered many and great difficulties, he has ever preserved an unsullied reputation, and, over the Spanish Main, the name of Richard Sheil is still a proverb of probity and soundness. But besides this valuable qualification, he brought to public life an intelligence strong and unshackled. In which, if occasionally there was in details a narrowness, there never was an obliquity of view humour abundant, ready, racy, and in the spoils of extensive satirical reading were happily blended with a produce of a rich original vein eloquence fluent, pleasing and often graceful. An enthusiasm for, and a trustfulness in the people, which is the surest characteristic of a robust political leader, whenever it is found combined with a well-sharpened judgement and a quick sense of the ridiculous.

But these rare qualifications were, for a long time, to a great extent, neutralised by the very prejudices against the more substantial operations of which Mr. Sheil's warfare was waged. His Catholicism told fearfully against him in his efforts in favour of reform, as well as those, which he made for religious liberty. One hardly knows whether to attribute the disappearance of nearly all this prejudice to the influence of Alderman Sheil's personal character, or to the successful results of his public labours.

The difficulties, which, in this respect, Mr. Sheil has overcome, throw a character over the whole of his life. We may compare the estimation in which Mr. Sheil has been held to that in which the public has, at different times, held Daniel O'Connell, long deemed a firebrand and a public enemy, there cannot be both of them, in their several degrees, a time when the hot labours of their busiest days were seen to have been guided by the purest and highest principles of natural justice and political enlightenment.

Happier than O'Connell, Mr. Sheil's latter days have fallen in a period of public tranquillity, and his position and the growing responsibilities of actual administration would have prevented him—if his natural temperament would not—from running into extremes or degenerating into wildness. He has wisely gone with the times. He has appreciated his success. He has seen Parliamentary Reform established and is, perhaps, not sorry, as the Conservatism which comes with old age, even to the strongest Liberals, creeps over him, that his own expectations from that great change have been. In some degree, as the ill prophecies of its opponents have been utterly disappointed.

In municipal affairs Mr. Sheil, after great exertion and after bravely receiving the bitterest odium, has seen the Corporation Schools thrown open to children of all sects, and the education so regulated that all may participate in it without risk of proselytism or other drawbacks to its advantages. He has lived to see two other respectable and respected members of his church take important and useful positions in the Town Council, and altogether to live in an atmosphere of liberality and kindness that, at one time, must have been wholly inconceivable to him.

To have filled such a role as Mr. Sheil's with honour and dignity is to have done far more than a public man on the other side can possibly achieve. A Tory and a Protestant may climb as high in Liverpool esteem as Mr. Sheil has climbed, but it is not from such a depth. It is easy for a top-sawyer to seem grand, and to get credit an under-sawyer must be a very good one indeed to win honour and no one is more an under-sawyer than a Liberal Catholic in Liverpool, even now, when prejudice has, to some extent, been dissipated.

Perhaps the criminal bar offers a better comparison. Every one knows how calm, impartial, graceful, and moderate a council can be who is frequently retained for the prosecution and whose practice is chiefly for the crown. Yet many a barrister has won a personal reputation for suavity, graciousness, and judicial acumen only because of the great afforded him by the accident of his business being of his character. The man however, who really deserves honour is he who, as council for the defence, is not more brilliant than cautious; not more eager for his client then just to those whom he is tempted to asperse on his client's behalf; not more ingenious than truthful; not more alive to the immortal principles of justice than to the necessity of protecting and purifying society. Such a man as Alderman Richard Sheil has been at the bar of public opinion.

He was long the volunteer attorney-general not

only for his oppressed and harassed co-religionists, but of the whole unrepresented population of his adopted town, and, so far as it fell within the scope of his opportunities, the advocate of every liberal and down-trodden interest in the country, and he has in this difficult character borne himself ever with dignity, truthfulness, candour, personal kindliness, and every other quality that can adorn the performance of an onerous and peculiarly riskful office.

In the council Mr. Sheil's style is pungent and terse, and his manner has always a sort of latent humour, a little dashed of late with the tetchiness and fussiness of age. He speaks with a rich, but gentlemanly soupcon of the brogue. He always takes what may be called the Finance Committee view of municipal questions, being, perhaps, a little flattered by his recent honours: but he has never yielded to the Finance Committee's weakness of siding with officials. It may be doubted whether Mr. Sheil shares those sensations of rapture with which it is the fashion to regard the staff of the Liverpool Corporation.

We fancy he supposes that they, as a rule, do as little as they can, get as much as they can, and go to London as often as they can. If these prejudices are unjust to our staff, they are certainly in accordance with general facts, which may excuse Mr. Sheil entertaining them strongly. But Mr. Sheil's administrative and deliberative characteristics will soon cease to be public topics, and he will be remembered not for the services he rendered in the purple of the Finance Deputy-Chairmanship, but for history and progress of liberality and the decay of bigotry and intolerance in Liverpool. His life will long bare fruit for such benefits blossom perennially, and reproduce themselves in rich abundance as society advances.

'The Porcupine' March 4 1871 reported the death of Mr. Richard Sheil aged 80 yrs at his home in Bankfields Road, West Derby Liverpool.

He was a leader of men thirty years ago and what his generation struggled for our generation enjoys. He brought to public affairs the prestige of an unstained private character, and throughout his career he had the same valuable anchor.

Mr. Sheil had for several years past ceased to take any active part in public affairs, but he never ceased to adorn a strongly attached private circle by his amiability, geniality, and warm-heartedness. He will long be remembered—not so much for his services that he rendered to the Town Council, but for those, which rendered the story of his most active years the history and progress of liberality and the decay of bigotry and intolerance in Liverpool. Although Richard Sheil was a very wealthy man who had a great love of Liverpool, he was always very proud of being a Tipperary man. On Saturday morning 6th March Richard Sheil was interred in the Roman Catholic portion of Anfield Cemetery, among those present were the Lord Mayor (Mr. J. G. Livingston) Mr. William Ewart Gladstone, and Michael James Whitty.

On the death of Richard Sheil the family business passed into the hands of his nephew Christopher James Corbally. Like his uncle, he was born in Ireland and came to Liverpool at an early age. His influences were used in connection with the introduction of Catholic reformatories. He, no doubt, felt such institutions would help to develop young people who had gone astray in a more positive way. Until four years before his death he filled the post of treasurer to the Catholic reformatory ship 'Clarence'. He also took a great interest in the Catholic Benevolent Society, holding the post of treasurer for a period of over thirty years. Christopher was also much respected in non-Catholic circles, and in 1857 he was elected as a Liberal member of the City Council for Vauxhall Ward, which he held until 1860, then raised to the magisterial bench the same year. His kindness, shrewdness, and intelligence whilst fulfilling the duties of a magistrate, gained him the esteem of all who were associated with him. Sixteen years after taking over the family business, the Catholic Family Annual and Almanac for the Diocese of Liverpool 1888 informed its readers of the death of Corbally.

Christopher James Corbally, of Bedford Street South, Liverpool, died on Friday, 2nd December 1887, in the 75th year of his age. Mr. Corbally came to Liverpool in early life from Ireland, and entered the office of his uncle, Mr. Richard Sheil, who was engaged in the West Indian Trade. Subsequently Mr. Corbally became a partner in the firm of Richard Sheil and Co., and the success which attended their transactions was due in a large measure to the careful business habits and ability of Mr. Corbally. He manifested a deep and active interest in all the Catholic charities of Liverpool and in fact in every movement, which had for its objective the improvement of the social position of his co-religionists.

Reference, was made to the good qualities of Christopher James Corbally at the Police Court by Mr. Charles Aspinall, J.P. and Sir James Picton.

Mr. Corbally's efforts on behalf of the poor did not terminate with his public labours. In his private life, he endeavoured to befriend them in every possible way and his charitable benefactions may be said to have been almost innumerable. The value of his labours on behalf of Catholicism in Liverpool was all the greater, because at the time when he threw himself into the struggle for the maintenance of their rights and the elevation of their social status, there were not many men in a position to give them a helping hand. His death which had not been unexpected, in as much as he had for some time been in failing health, caused most sincere regret amongst a wide circle of friends.

Christopher James Corbally was buried in Anfield Cemetery alongside the family graves of Richard Sheil and Michael James Whitty.

4

James Muspratt
and his sons

James Muspratt

James Muspratt (1793-1886) was one of those brilliant and outstanding Irishmen who chose to make their mark in business in the thriving port of Liverpool during the early part of the nineteenth-century. Born 12 August 1793, in Dublin, he became a druggist's apprentice, and then served in both the Army and Navy in the Peninsular War (a struggle carried out by Great Britain as the ally of Spain and Portugal against France, 1808-1814). After his release from the forces, and having received a small inheritance in 1818, he manufactured various chemicals in a small way in Dublin.

In 1823 Muspratt moved his business to Liverpool and sited it on the banks of the Leeds and Liverpool Canal in the Vauxhall area, where he began to make soda by the Leblanc process. The people living in Vauxhall at that time would have been in the main agricultural workers and small manufacturers, yet it was only four years after Muspratt's arrival that the 'Liverpool Mercury' published a letter dated 5th October 1827, which read:

Regarding the chemical works such volumes of sulphurous smoke as to darken the whole atmosphere in the neighbourhood, so much so that the Church of St. Martin-in-the-Field can not be seen from the houses at about one hundred yards distance, the stones of which are already turned a dark colour, from the cause. The scent is almost insufferable, as well as injurious to the health of persons residing in the neighbourhood.

James Muspratt was becoming a force in the chemical industry when he moved part of his operations from Vauxhall and opened factories to make sulphuric acid at St. Helens and Widnes, two small towns close to Liverpool. As he was a friend of Justus Baron Von Liebig 1803-1873, the German chemist, he undertook the manufacture of super-phosphates and artificial manures, which had been invented by Liebig.

It must have been a very exciting time for the young James Muspratt when we look at what that industry produced during and after the early part of the nineteenth-century. The business of using chemical reactions to turn raw materials, such as coal, oil, and salt, into a variety of products brought about many technological advances in the chemical industry and dramatically altered the world's economy. James Muspratt was a visionary who helped in the creation of that vast industry.

As Muspratt's industry expanded, so did his influence in the world of the chemical industry and he is known worldwide as one of its fathers. By this time he had settled well into his new adopted town of Liverpool. He built a villa in Bootle, a few miles down river from Liverpool, some time during the late 1820s. In 1835 he bought a large house in Pembroke Place in the centre of the town. Again he did not remain long in this new house as he missed the sight of the Mersey with its fleet of sailing vessels inward and outward bound. He also missed the enjoyment of the ever-changing face of the river and made up his mind to live closer to it, when he had the means to do so. Having bought twenty acres on the shore at Seaforth, he was determined to build a house of noble dimensions and classic style on land that consisted of nothing but sand-hills. In 1839 he laid the foundation stone of his mansion, Seaforth Hall, designed in the classical Greek style by the Liverpool architect and historian, Sir James Picton.

In order to give constant attention to the building of his new home and laying out the grounds, James Muspratt rented a house nearby for a short time. It was a vicarage in the grounds of Seaforth House, built by John Gladstone, father of Prime Minister, Mr. William Ewart Gladstone. James Muspratt's new house standing out solitary on the shoreline was a very noticeable building and used to be a landmark for passengers from New York. Ellen Terry, a leading actress of the day, once remarked to a friend that she looked forward to the site of the Greek Mansion which stood on the banks of the Mersey as a first glimpse of home.

Many of James Muspratt's houseguests were scientific, theatrical and literary figures of the day. Among them were Charles Dickens, Samuel Lover and Michael James Whitty. The terrible tragedy of the Irish Famine of 1845-1849 led to many discussions as to the cause of the potato disease. Baron Von Liebig had been consulted on the subject and had expressed a desire to visit Ireland. James Muspratt arranged a small group of friends to go with him. This consisted of Edmond Knowles Muspratt, his youngest son, Samuel Lover, novelist and songwriter, Michael James Whitty, a Wexford man, editor of the 'Liverpool Journal' and founder of the 'Liverpool Daily Post', and Mr. Fincham, manager of the British Plate Glass Company in St. Helens. The visit was extremely interesting and Whitty published an account in the 'Liverpool Journal'. Unfortunately, a copy does not appear to be in existence.

Muspratt's party hoped to call on Sir Robert Kane who was principal of the new University College of Cork, but on arrival they found he was not in the city so decided not to visit the college. Muspratt and his friends travelled to Galway to see Connemara, which they regarded as being the poorest part of Ireland. They also felt part of the cause of the suffering of the people was the breakdown of the landlord system as a result of which the large estates were either sold or put up for sale.

There was no railway further than Athlone, so they had to avail themselves of the Bianconi public cars and had the pleasure of using this pioneer mode of travel. These cars travelled at the rate of eight or ten miles an hour. Edmond Knowles Muspratt complained, "However much they might suit local people who were accustomed to the outside Irish car, foreigners found them very tiring, and difficult to prevent themselves falling off when going at a high speed. So after a long day's journey we sought another mode of conveyance, and had to put up with a couple of post-chaises". (A carriage usually with four wheels to carry two or four people, a popular name was po'chay). Nevertheless they enjoyed the trip, as Edmond wrote:

> The scenery in Connemara is very fine and the bays very picturesque, and Lover, with the eye of an artist, drew our attention to the most beautiful views, and the strikingly interesting girls with their picturesque costumes and red petticoats. These young girls are beautiful, with features, which denote the admixture of Spanish blood, derived from the time when Galway and the South of Ireland had a large and lucrative trade with the Peninsula and Mediterranean, all destroyed by the English rule, the destruction being completed by the Union. Under Home Rule much of this prosperity may revive. We returned to Dublin, to visit County Wicklow, and then came back to Liverpool.

Samuel Lover was one of James Muspratt's closest

friends, and frequently stayed with the family at Seaforth. An Irish novelist and songwriter, he wrote 'Legends and Stories of Ireland', which he illustrated himself. He was also a miniaturist and dramatist. Born in Dublin Feb. 24, 1797, he became Secretary of the Royal Hibernian Academy in 1830. He helped to fund the 'Dublin University Magazine' in 1835. He moved to London the same year, hoping to secure a larger clientele for his work. There he painted a beautiful miniature of Paganini and was so pleased with it that he would not part with it during his life. When Lover's effects were sold after his death, Edmond Knowles purchased the miniature and a few other items of importance. Lover was also associated with Dickens in the establishment of Bentley's 'Miscellany' in 1837. He had to abandon painting through failing eyesight. He gave recitals, which he called Irish evenings, in London, Canada and the United States in the years 1846-1848. He wrote 'Rory O'More', a national romance in 1837, 'Handy Andy', 1842 and 'He Would Be A Gentleman' in 1844, but he was best remembered for his ballads, 'Rory O'More', 'The Low Backed Car', 'The Angel's Whisper', 'The Four Leafed Shamrock', 'Molly Bawn' and 'Widow Machree'. He wrote the music as well as the words of his songs and it was said he sang them with excellent effect. He died at St. Helier Jersey July 6, 1868 and was buried at Kensal Green, London.

James Muspratt's eldest son, James Sheridan Muspratt was also a chemist born in Dublin March 18, 1821. He studied chemistry at Glasgow and University College, London. He took a post under Liebig at Giessen Germany, where he carried out researches on sulphites, toluidine, and nitraniline. Returning to England, he settled in Liverpool.

Leading the way for his younger brothers, he worked first with Justus von Liebig in Giessen and later with August von Hofmann. In 1841 James Sheridan Muspratt founded the Liverpool College of Chemistry, which was modelled on Hofmann's innovative Royal College of

Chemistry in London. He was a prolific author and it is for his 1857-60 two-volume 'Chemistry, Theoretical, Practical and Analytical' that his name became known worldwide. His work was translated into Russian and German.

Just like his father, James Sheridan, he developed an interest in the arts and this brought him into contact with Charles Dickens, who became a close friend of the Muspratt family. Sheridan Muspratt was the Hon. Secretary of an amateur dramatic society and on July 28th 1847 Charles Dickens called on the amateur actors to appear at the Theatre Royal, Williamson Square, Liverpool, in a performance of 'Every Man In His Humour'. William Charles Macready, actor and manager, and many other literary and theatrical luminaries were invited to stay at the home of the Muspratts in Seaforth. Sheridan's friendship with people in the art world also brought him into contact with Susan Cushman, a well-known actress who later became his wife.

The Muspratts delighted in entertaining some of the best names in British society at Seaforth Hall, or at garden parties on the lawns of their country estate. It was observed that:

> Seaforth Hall took in a wide view of the Welsh Mountains, the perfection of its lawns and gardens typified the elegance of Liverpool's wealthiest class. With its fogs and the black smoke polluting its skies, Liverpool might leave much to be desired, but flowered estates like Seaforth were regal paradises and meeting James Sheridan Muspratt was the shining event of many who were invited to Seaforth Hall. James Sheridan Muspratt died in Liverpool in February 1851.

It was Edmond Knowles Muspratt, the youngest son, who was the driving force in the family business during his father's advancing years. He was born in Bootle, the district then called Bootle-Cum-Linacre, on November

6th, 1833, at his father's house on the shores of the Mersey, close to the old Bootle landmarks, two obelisks which served to direct ships coming up the river. Many years later, in his eightieth year, while writing his memoir, he described the scene as it was at that time:

> Warehouses and railway-sidings standing on the sites where primroses once abounded for the city has crept up to our garden walls and the Gladstone Dock has now been built on land adjoining the Seaforth Hall Grounds. When the Aquitania or other big liners are in dock they overshadow practically the whole landscape and seem to sit on our front lawn. The Gladstone Dock, be it noted, was not called after the great statesman, but after Mr. Robert Gladstone of Dock Board fame.

Throughout their lives James Muspratt and his family retained a great affection for Ireland the country of their birth. But it was this youngest son, Edmond Knowles Muspratt, born in Bootle, who being a successful businessman, also became a political activist, and as a Liverpool born Irishman wrote:

> In Liverpool the Irish question had always taken a prominent part in all elections, and Lord Ramsay, in 1879, who stood as the Liberal candidate, accepted the principal of Home Rule for Ireland. But in 1880 he succeeded to the peerage as Lord Dalhousie on his father's death. The year 1879 being very wet, led to serious depression in agriculture in both England and Ireland, and it was necessary for the Government to deal with the land question, as the eviction of tenants from their holdings, owing to their inability to pay any rent, had led to serious agrarian disturbances and outrages.
>
> To meet the immediate difficulties, the Irish Secretary Mr. W. E. Forster, brought in a compensation for disturbance Bill, to the House of Commons which was rejected by the House of Lords. This rejection

strengthened the hands of Mr. Parnell, who, at the head of a large body of Home Rulers, was able by obstruction of all kinds to place difficulties in the way of the Government. In Ireland the Land League was formed to support the tenants who refused to pay rent, which many found impossible owing to the agricultural depression.

The Government brought in a 'Land Bill' that set up courts to decide what was a fair rent, it also embodied compensation for disturbance, rejected by the House of Lords, for security of tenure to the tenant. Many Liberals were opposed to this policy of coercion, which had been frequently tried without success in the past, and, to use the words of John Bright, "force was no remedy". Personally I was strongly against the Coercion Bill, and when a meeting was held in Liverpool, called especially by workingmen, I would have attended if I had not been too late, as shown by the following correspondence:

"Sir I venture to enclose an invitation to a meeting to be held on Saturday. The meeting has been organised by persons not directly connected with either political party, who suspect Coercion even when it is supported by both sides of the House of Commons.

You have the reputation of being an independent politician who has always placed the cause of freedom above the interests of faction, and we ask you to sustain this reputation by being present at Saturday's meeting, even if you do not care to speak. I am, Sir, On behalf of the organisers of the meeting, A Compton."

Edmond Knowles replied to the invitation and left no doubt as to his true feelings towards the injustice perpetrated against the people of Ireland when he wrote:

I am obliged for your invitation to attend Anti-Coercion meeting to be held tomorrow. Personally I am of the opinion that the Government has made a mistake in introducing a Bill for the suspension of the

Habeas Corpus Act in Ireland at the present time. As such action ought only to be taken in a country that boasts of its freedom, as a last resort and when no other means is likely to attain the end desired of making the law respected. Such a case cannot be held, to be made out until the main cause of the disturbance, viz. Bad laws, have been reformed.

During the period 1880 to 1890 Edmond Knowles Muspratt was very actively engaged in politics. He was chairman of the Liverpool Reform Club from 1883 to 1884 and also president of the Liberal Association of Widnes, as there was a large Irish population in that town. He was a member of the town council for St. Peters Ward, from 1880 to 1885. He was also interested in the extension of the franchise in the counties and in Home Rule for Ireland. He presided at many large meetings of the Liberal Association, giving special attention to, as well as promoting interest in, the question of land tenure in both England and Ireland.

His views on the land question were well known, for as President of the Financial Reform Association he had advocated the taxation of land values and security for the tenant. In 1884 the Bill for the extension of the franchise in the counties and a redistribution of seats was carried, and the Widnes Division of South West Lancashire obtained the right to return a member at the General Election of 1885. Owing to some difference of opinion in the Liberal Party, there was some difficulty finding a suitable candidate and Muspratt was encouraged to accept the position, on the grounds that he was the only person likely to unite the sections. Much against his desire he finally consented to stand, and sent a letter of acceptance, which read:

Taking part in public affairs in Liverpool and Widnes, and from the unanimity of the vote in the District Councils, I gather that they are generally acceptable to the Liberal Party in the Division. My political opinions are, I believe, generally known to you, as I have taken an active part in public affairs in Liverpool and Widnes. With respect to Ireland, which must necessarily engage the attention of the coming Parliament, I have always sympathised with the aspirations of her people towards Home Rule, and have consistently deprecated a policy of coercion. I am Dear Sir, Your faithful servant, Edmund K. Muspratt.

During the election year 1885 Muspratt felt Mr. Parnell and the Irish Nationalists were foolish enough to believe they could get better terms from the Tories than from Mr. Gladstone and the Liberal Government, who were not able to promise an absolute suspension of coercion in Ireland. Mr. Parnell and the Irish Nationalist party, relying upon the professions of the Tories, had decided at the General Election, in all English constituencies, to call upon his followers to support the Tory candidate, as opposed to the Liberals. This policy, it was thought had a disastrous effect in the Widnes Division, and Muspratt wrote:

For although I had been a strong Home Ruler, and would have voted with the Irish party on this question, orders were given to all the Irish electors to vote for the Tory candidate. I may here mention a characteristic speech made by my old friend Mr. T. P. O'Connor on this occasion. Coming up to me later, "Tay Pay" pressed my hand and said with impressments, referring to his fellow Irishmen and their orders from headquarters: "We have got to vote against you, Mr. Muspratt, but it breaks my hear-r-r-rts to do it." Personally I think this was a mistake on the part of Parnell, and I think the Irish party have since seen that had they supported Mr. Gladstone at that election Home Rule would have been carried by a large majority in the English House of Commons, and a fight in the House of Lords would have taken place much earlier, and the Radical party in England would have been strengthened. But Mr. Gladstone had other difficulties to contend with, as Mr. Chamberlain started his unauthorised programme, which he propounded at Warrington, and caused some difficulties in the Liberal party at Widnes, where of course I was defeated. Ever since Widnes has returned a Tory member.

Edmond Knowles recalls Liverpool and the surrounding area in a period we today can never hope to understand except through the eyes of people like the Muspratt's who lived through those times:

I have only pleasant recollections of my time spent during the building of Seaforth Hall, and my daily amusement was riding my pony on the shore to a small cottage which, being the last house until you come to Southport, we christened 'The Worlds End'. There were at that time in Church Road in the Waterloo area only three or four houses and no houses between Waterloo and Seaforth except 'Potters Barn'. Describing the dock area Edmond Knowles Muspratt wrote. "In the direction of Liverpool the shore extended to what is now the Stanley Dock, a distance of three miles, and in fine weather many of the residents of the neighbourhood rode into town (Liverpool) on horseback, instead of taking the canal boat from Litherland, or driving along the recently made road parallel with the shore, passing through two toll bars". The new road was Regent Road commonly known as the Dock Road and this was at a time before the line of docks from the Stanley Dock to Seaforth was constructed. Muspratt, still describing the journey into Liverpool. "Along the road were several good houses or villas, in the district called Bootle Marsh, and there were at intervals, roads leading down to houses leading down to the shore. Among these was one built in castellated form, by Mr. Miller, and called 'Millers Castle'. Mr. Miller was well known in Liverpool and Bootle, besides giving his name to the castle, he also built a bridge over the canal, and when the Southport railway was open in 1848 or 1849, the bridge was named Millers Bridge.

Today there are no visible signs of the Seaforth, described by Edmond Knowles Muspratt. He died in the home that he loved, 'Seaforth Hall' on the 1st September 1923 aged 89 years. James Muspratt died in Liverpool, May 4, 1886. There now stands on the site of 'Seaforth Hall' a large mill close to Gladstone Dock. Sir Max Muspratt, carried on the pioneering work of his grandfather, James Muspratt, was Chairman of United Alkali Co Ltd and in 1924 became a director of the giant ICI Company.

Sir Max Muspratt

5

Michael James Whitty

---His mannerisms of style, few leader-writers in or out of London ever equalled Mr. Whitty for power of vivid colouring, none was always so readable—his rapid flow of epigrammatic wisdom and original axioms carrying all before him.

'Liverpool Daily Post', September 1872

Very few people in Liverpool will stop to inquire how the Liverpool Police Force came into being, or how Liverpool's 'Daily Post' newspaper first appeared on the newsstand in 1855. This was due to one man, Michael James Whitty born in Nicharee, Duncormick, Co. Wexford in 1795, son of a farmer, maltster and ship owner, in the port of Wexford. He became a journalist, police chief and a newspaper proprietor more or less in that order.

He was allowed to share lessons with his eldest brother who was destined for the church and had a private tutor in Greek and Latin. Michael received his education at St. Peter's College, Wexford and at an early age he became his father's assistant, but unfortunately the business failed.

He moved to Dublin in 1821, where he commenced his literary career and it was here that he was to meet, and later marry, Mary O'Neill. A short while after his marriage they moved to London, where he became a journalist. In 1823 he was appointed editor of the 'London and Dublin Magazine', where he remained until 1827. In the first volume of the magazine, there appeared an article on 'Robert Emmet' (1778-1803) the leader of the 1798 rebellion in Ireland

During this time he contributed largely to Irish periodical literature, and was an ardent advocate for Catholic emancipation. In 1822-24 he published two volumes of 'Tales of Irish Life', illustrative of the manners, customs and condition of the people, with illustrations by his friend George Cruickshank. An extract from the preface of 'Tales of Irish Life' informs us:

An elegant modern writer has remarked that Englishmen have more accurate information respecting countries situated at the extremity of the globe than those nearer home. Approximation he has represented as unfavourable to truth and candor. Should it be argued that this assertion is too general, it must be admitted to be too true in one instance; for less is actually known in this country of the Real State of Ireland than of the regions beyond the Ganges and Mississippi. Native writers, from a false patriotism, have exaggerated and distorted facts while foreigners, from prejudice and ignorance, have dealt largely in misrepresentations. The public inquires, and are deceived, till by degrees falsehood acquires the consistency of truth; and too many English readers (like theatrical amateurs) are only pleased with representations of Irish life where nature, truth, and common sense, are outraged and insulted – where things are done and said which are as foreign to Ireland as they are to Hinduism.

Michael was great admirer of Shakespeare, Oisin, Lord Byron and Moore and many other poets and the following poem is an example of the poetry of Thomas Moore, born Dublin, on the 28th May 1779.

Come, tell me where the maid is found,
Whose heart can love without deceit?
And I will rang the world around,
To sigh one moment at her feet.

Oh! Tell me where's her sainted, home,
What air receives her blessed sigh?
A pilgrimage of years I'll roam
To catch one sparkle of her eye.

Tom Moore

Using a pseudonym 'Captain Rock', Michael published 'Captain Rock' in London or the 'Chieftains Weekly Gazette' for the year 1825 and 'Captain Rock' or 'The Chieftains Gazette for the year 1827'. Once more Michael moved on in 1828, this time to Liverpool, which was an expanding town. It was the home of the British shipping industry in its golden age of shipping. Up the river to the docks of the River Mersey came the produce of the world and most especially American cotton for the mills of Lancashire. Down-stream with the tide flowed all the manufactured goods of the Midlands and the industrial North.

Michael accepted the post of editor of the newly formed 'Liverpool Journal' in 1830 and he continued as editor until 1833. It was at this time that a dramatic change came about in Michael's life. It seemed to be out of character when he put to one side his journalistic skills, for what appeared to be an alien way of life.

He was appointed to the post of Superintendent of the Night Watch. His duties were to organize a band of untrained and badly disciplined men, whose job it was to carry out police duties for the Corporation. They consisted of 170 old and decrepit night watchmen and

52 Exchange Police. Michael was a very big and powerful man and stood no nonsense from his men, but even with his stature he was glad of a helping hand at times, and he stayed in this post for three years. J. A. Picton, in his 'Memorials of Liverpool' wrote:

> The anniversary of the battle of the Boyne occurred on Sunday. It was expected that the Orangemen would make a grand demonstration, but if such was intended, it was prevented by the occurrences, which took place. Collections of lower classes of Irish assembled in the streets at the north end of the town and about ten at night a fracas took place in Ben Johnson Street, which led to the capture of one of the ringleaders by the police. This was the signal for a general row. The mob set upon the watchman, rescued the prisoners and assaulted the officers so hotly that they were driven from the street.
>
> Another commotion arose in Great Crosshall Street and the two mobs uniting, being fifty-to-one, as compared with the officers, the latter were compelled to take flight and seek refuge in the lock-up in Vauxhall Road. The rioters proceeded to break it down with axes and staves, with loud cheers and outcries from an assembled crowd. Those inside barricaded the inner doors and retreated to the loft, where the alarm fire-bell was sounded. Mr. Whitty, the head of the night police, hearing the bell, drove at once to the station, where he was attacked with the utmost violence. Being a powerful man, he contended boldly with his assailants, but it might have gone hard with him had it not been for two young men amongst the rioters who gallantly espoused his cause and assisted him to dash through the door, which had just been broken open. The rioters then paused as if uncertain what to do next, and assistance having in the meantime arrived, the mob were gradually forced back and in their turn forced to flee.
>
> On Monday morning the riots were renewed. A

large crowd assembled in Park Lane. Mr. Parlour, the chief constable endeavoured to persuade them to disperse, with the assurance that no Orange procession would be permitted, but the multitude increasing, the dock police were sent for and a detachment of the 80th regiment was called out to clear the streets. The mob, driven from Park Lane, proceeded to Vauxhall Road, where they joined another body already assembled. The nightly watch were again called out and a hundred special constables sworn in and dispatched to the scene. Although there was great excitement during the day, no further emeute took place. Many of the rioters were taken into custody, on whom were found pistols, with powder and ball and other deadly weapons. The most active of them were tried and punished.

Michael had served his apprenticeship well with his part time Night Watch duties. In 1835, the Liverpool Watch Committee, as a result of the 1832 Reform Act, approached him and offered him the post of Head Constable. Thus not only was he Liverpool's first Head Constable, but also the founder of the Police Force and Fire Brigade in Liverpool. As Head Constable he was regarded as the first full-time senior permanent official of the Corporation, and the Police Force itself was the first large body of municipal employees. The town Police Body was organised on February 29, 1836, and consisted of 290 men, 24 inspectors and four superintendents, plus 40 fire-police men, bridewell keepers and indoor officers. About twelve months later the dock police was amalgamated with the town police.

Michael's first love was journalism and after eleven years in this post as Chief Constable he retired on the 22nd January 1847. On his retirement the town council presented him with the sum of £1000. This allowed him to devote the rest of his life to journalism. Not that he ever ceased to be a journalist, his connection with the 'Liverpool Journal' had not been wholly severed during his service with the Liverpool Police Force.

In 1848 Michael went on to purchase the 'Liverpool Journal', which had its premises at 18 Castle Street. He advocated the abolition of the stamp act on newspapers, and other forms of duty on newspapers. When a committee was appointed to enquire into the effect of duties on paper and advertisements, (usually called taxes on knowledge) Whitty, in giving evidence, said that if they were repelled he would publish a daily paper priced at one penny. The price of a newspaper at that time was between three to six pence. On the repeal of these taxes, in 1855 he founded the 'Liverpool Daily Post', the first penny daily paper published in the United Kingdom. Other Liverpool newspapers were also reduced to a penny, which made the competition more aggressive, as there were two Liberal newspapers and only one Conservative newspaper in a town, which was politically Tory.

In 1851, Ramshay, a judge of Preston County Court, made some scathing criticism of Liverpool people. He was overbearing and tyrannical, and Whitty attacked him in a searing editorial. Michael was summoned by two bailiffs to appear before the judge. His admirers filled the courthouse and interrupted the proceedings with cheering and jeers so the judge called the bailiffs to arrest those responsible. The bailiffs replied that they could not arrest the entire court, so the judge fined the bailiffs five pounds for incompetence.

After a sensational trial, Michael was fined but he refused to pay the fine and was escorted by a cheering crowd to serve seven days in Lancaster jail. His fine and that of the bailiffs was paid by his friends and the mob escorted him home again. Over two thousand signatures of notable people of all denominations were collected for a petition, for the removal of the Judge. After a hearing lasting several days the Judge was dismissed and faced hundreds of pounds in legal costs.

The commencement of the Civil War in the United States brought about a situation which compelled people to support one side or the other. Michael boldly took the side of the federal Government, when the governing classes in England, and the majority of commercial men in Liverpool, espoused the cause of the South after cotton became scarce. Curiously enough, this had very little effect on the sale of the paper, and shows that the mass of the people took a different view from that of wealthier classes.

Michael also produced 'Whitty's Guide to Liverpool' in 1868, and it was not long after this that the 'Liverpool Daily Post' passed out of his hands, and the rest of his life was spent in retirement at his home in Prince's Park, Liverpool. With the parting of Michael James Whitty hardly anything beyond the change in the imprint of the paper indicated a change of owner. For some months before Michael's departure he had ceased to play a part in the production of the paper because of poor health. 'The Porcupine' wrote:

> The local newspaper press is not so overstocked with original ability that the final retirement of "the father of the penny press" as he likes to call himself and be called, should take place without a public, if informal, acknowledgement of the hard work he has performed in the pioneership of popular papers.

The 'Daily Post' was not the first established of the provincial dailies, the 'Northern Daily Times' claimed that distinction, but the 'Liverpool Daily Post' was to prove the power of the almighty Penny. It was able to claim credit of establishment of cheap outlets for public opinion in every centre of the population outside of London. The influence of Whitty to bring the penny press to the poor man was to give him a wider view of the world and the right to examine those in power. 'The Porcupine' went on to write:

> To take from the men in power has been, and generally for good, it is too late in the day to insist

45

upon. It is the Archimedean lever to move the world, and only an extensive circulation is needed as the fulcrum. Mightier than the sword, the leader writer's pen had most materially helped to make and unmake dynasties, alter maps, provoke wars, and effect complete revolutions in social and political life. The daily paper is no longer the luxury it once was, some would say it is a necessity of civilized life. Sitting at his breakfast table, every man has in his penny paper a camera obscura, or reduced photograph, of all the events taking place throughout the world. All the great inventions by which the present century has been signalised are specially subsidised for the favourite daily, which combines a general post office, telegraph station, railway terminus, and news centre all in one, and, as the showmen say, all for the low charge of one penny.

Michael had his critics and would often be reminded of frequent errors and indiscretions associated with his journal. He had to walk a tight rope at times in the way he reported events in his adopted town, a town close to his heart. He was an Irishman who had been in a position of power almost from the first day he entered Liverpool and had always played the part of honest broker, both as a policeman and newspaper proprietor. 'The Porcupine', recorded Michael's retirement from his beloved 'Liverpool Daily Post' in September 1872.

Of the vast beneficial results, which have followed the propagation of penny papers throughout the provinces, Mr. M. J. Whitty is fairly entitled to claim credit as the leader in the van. Through every vicissitude of fortune, till success was realised, he pluckily stuck to his post, and seemed wishful to "die with harness on his back," but no doubt friendly counsels have prevailed in persuading him that, after so busy a career, he has a right to seek rest in the twilight of age.

Having all the proverbial determination, courage, and independence of a Wexford man, the varied and peculiar experience of a chief constable, the ripeness of a widely-read scholar, and the adjuncts of an original, often bizarre style, a mental magazine of out-of-the-way facts, and an inclination to ride to death social hobbies which were often the merest "screws"— Mr. Whitty undertook to superadd to the success of the well-established journal the onerous duties of the editor of a daily paper, and, for the last seventeen years, has almost every morning given us his views on things "in general and particular." With the peculiarities of his style we are all very familiar.

He was nothing if not dogmatic – daringly dictatorial, but always infallible. If he told you twice two made five, he would do it with such an air of confidence in the statement that you could not question it. If in almost the same breath, with that sententious gravity which always overawed, he told you that twice two made three, you dare hardly doubt the arithmetic. Then, having settled the statistics by a simple statement (unfounded on fact), he would proceed with graphic force to rear a superstructure of inconsequent arguments, original aphorisms, and perhaps striking paradoxes, piled on with a power that prevented you testing the falsity of the foundation of his premises. When he had completed his fanciful architecture, he would complacently admire the beauty and strength of his deductions, and challenge you to find a flaw.

His memorable and triumphant tussle with all the Celtic weakness for a scrimmage, from the time of the eccentric Ramshay, the County Court Judge, he was ever ready to try political, social and ecclesiastical conclusions with any competitor, great or small, and, having the advantage of the first blood and the last word, he could generally manage to leave a mark behind his literary shillelagh.

His mannerisms of style, few leader-writers in or

out of London ever equalled Mr. Whitty for power of vivid colouring, none was always so readable – his rapid flow of epigrammatic wisdom and original axioms carrying all before him. On many great social questions he displayed a true grasp of the subject, an intuitive and rare power of regarding it in a broad liberal light from all points of view simultaneously. It will ever rebound to the credit of his foresight that, with only one or two other papers in the kingdom, the 'Liverpool Daily' Post persistently and to the end, through good and evil repute, and at the risk of its popularity, where the Southern interest so strong, upheld the cause of the North in the American civil struggle, and even when the war-clouds hung heaviest, predicted the final triumph of the side he so boldly championed.

Of Mr. Whitty's use of his local influence we can honestly speak in favourable terms. Though his good nature often led him to indulge in superfluous praise of men and things in which the public had no special interest. His pen was always freely at the service of every cause that commended itself to genuine charity, and was not slow at times to scourge the social abuses with which unfortunately, our local life is far too rife. If Mr.Whitty, instead of devoting his pen almost exclusively to the necessarily short, hurried, and versatile essays required for a daily paper, had expended the mental power and varied intellectual resources, of which he is the undoubted possessor, on work of a more deliberate and enduring nature, he must have attained a high place in modern literature.

The ephemeral character of newspaper work, the obligation 'to say something about everything', to cram for facts on occasion, and, above all, to conceal your ignorance on subjects wherein you are not quite at home, is fatal to the birth of productions that will live long. What is read today if forgotten to-morrow. Why write for to-morrow, therefore? The anonymity in which the pressman is shrouded is another great obstacle to work being produced for posterity.

In many ways Michael James Whitty's penny 'Journal' continued the work of the Mechanics Institutes, in bringing a wider picture of the world to those who could not afford the 'Times'. Mainly middle-class radicals and philanthropists, catering for the self-improvement among skilled workers founded the mechanics institutes. They provided Libraries, reading rooms and courses of lectures in the arts and sciences. Kitty Wilkinson, that great Liverpool philanthropist was a firm believer in the mechanics institutes and after 1850 mechanics institutes everywhere gradually lost ground to libraries and more specialized institutions of higher education. Michael brought not just his penny 'Journal' to the people of Liverpool he also he encouraged them to be proud of their expanding seaport and town on the banks of the River Mersey.

When Michael first entered Liverpool he set up home in 3 Everton Hill and later he moved to 1 Gambier Terrace. His last move was to a house he had built, 6 Princes Park Terrace. Amongst the treasured possessions he took with him to his new home was a plaster bust of Garibaldi, the Father of Italian Freedom. 'The Liverpool Daily Post' is no longer a broadsheet but it is still a well loved paper in the Liverpool and North Wales area and refuses to get involved in the sensationalism often attributed to most tabloid newspapers. Margaret Webster, great grand-daughter of Michael James Whitty recalls him having said:

I was very ambitious and I had a very exalted opinion of myself. I almost looked down on Homer and thought very little of Dr. Johnson. At an early age I devoted myself to the press and I now find that the pursuit was a noble one, a great one and a proud one. He maintained all his life that the press was the instrument of liberty, freedom and progress all over the world.

He believed that everyone connected with a

newspaper, from the editor to the messenger boys, should combine to use the press for the public good. Having made a name in the journalistic world of London, he was offered the editorship of a projected paper in Liverpool, 'The Journal'. He brought out the first number in 1830.

Two of Michael's fourteen children chose their father's profession to became respected journalists in their own right. One of them, Edward Michael Whitty, was the London correspondent of the 'Liverpool Journal'. His friends sometimes knew him as Ned Wexford. Alfred Whitty was the other journalist in the family and father of the actress Dame May Whitty. Two of Michael's daughters Anna and Sarah, looked after him during his remaining years. They were intelligent women, talented in music and literature, Anna wrote a novel and many short stories. Michael died at his home in Prince's Park on 10 June 1873, and was buried at Anfield Cemetery in the family grave.

6

George Fosbery Lyster

Who was this man?

The name Jesse Hartley is a name that comes easily to mind to many Liverpool people as he was the engineer in charge of the building of the Liverpool docks, but the name of George Fosbery Lyster is one that may not be recalled quite so easily when people discuss the erection of the docks. George Fosbery Lyster, born on the 7th September, 1821, at Mount Talbot, Co. Roscommon, Ireland, was the third son of Colonel Anthony Lyster, formerly of the 23rd Light Dragoons, from Lysterfield and Bushey Park, Co. Roscommon. His mother was the daughter of George Fosbery, of Clorane, Co. Limerick.

George Lyster had quite a pedigree, his ancestors having gone to Ireland from England in the reign of Queen Elizabeth and having done good service to the state, they were rewarded with large grants of land, mostly in the County of Roscommon. George Lyster was related to Sir Maurice Fitzgerald Bart, Knight of Kerry and also Fitzgerald, the Knight of the Glen, Sir John Leslie Bart of Glasslough who was M. P. for County

Monaghan and he was also related to the Marquis of Waterford and Sir John Nugent, Bart, of Cloncoskoran, County Waterford.

George was educated at King William's College, Isle of Man and at a private school and although he was at one time marked out for the army, circumstances ultimately decided his selection of engineering as a profession. He served his apprenticeship under Mr. James Meadows Rendal. Soon after completion of his apprenticeship, he was given a government appointment as an Assistant Resident Engineer on the works for the improvement of the River Shannon, in Ireland. After two years in this position he resigned to take what was considered a more important one in England, under his former chief, Mr. Rendal, with whom he remained until the latter's death. George married Martha E. Sanderson, 5 October 1848. (After her death he remarried Blanche Maude, 21 June 1898.)

Subsequent to Lyster's return to England, at a period when railway schemes were rife, he was engaged in parliamentary, railway, harbour and dock engineering. On the commencement of the great harbour of refuge, carried out by the Government at Holyhead, he was appointed Assistant Resident Engineer and made the original survey. After seven years at Holyhead, in 1853, he was appointed by the Government of Guernsey, Resident Engineer to the new harbour works at St. Peter Port. It was here that Mr Randel died in 1856 and upon his demise. George was appointed his successor as Engineer-in-Chief of those works.

His next engagement brought him to the Port of Liverpool in 1861. He was unanimously selected from among seventy competitors as Engineer-in-Chief to the Liverpool and Birkenhead Dock Estate and was also appointed Engineer to the Wallasey Embankment Commissioners. George Lyster's contribution to the development of the Port of Liverpool was exceptional and all the work he was involved in is listed at the end of this chapter. As the line of docks along the Mersey shore at Liverpool extended and particularly when the north and south ends of the Dock Estate became the site of the principle docks, a better form of transportation was needed. The old slow running horse omnibuses, which used the lines of the docks railway, had outlived their usefulness and in the year 1877, George Lyster designed and submitted to the board a scheme for giving better transport by means of an elevated railway above the roads as there was no space available for quick traffic at street level. The last plan, which Lyster prepared, was one for an electric overhead railway on iron columns which was carried out by the Overhead Railway Company.

George Lyster's plans were the first to be submitted and the Overhead Railway was opened in 1893.

Maintenance of much of this great work was neglected over the war years between 1939-45 but the Overhead Railway will always be part of Liverpool's great history and folklore. George Lyster was awarded the Knight of the Foreign Order of Leopold, having been elected to that honour by His Majesty, the King of the Belgians. This was for services rendered as one of the English commissioners, in conjunction with the then President of the Institution of Civil Engineers, in connection with the important harbour works carried out on the Belgian coast. George Lyster became known as the Emperor of Engineers for his work on the docks.

An example of Lyster's work can still be seen at the Albert Dock where warehouses standing on the edge of the dock and overlooking the water show the solid strength of Lyster's work. In recent years they have been converted into luxury flats.

On the Birkenhead and Wallasey side of the river Mersey, among the more important works designed and carried out by him, were the Birkenhead docks. They were designed and carried through Parliament by Mr. John B. Hartley, but subsequently altered on George Lyster's recommendation, by the closing of the great Low Water Basin (which after trial had proved a failure), and forming it into what is now the Wallasey Docks.

Other works attributed to George Lyster were: The Morpeth Branch Dock in lieu of the Open Tidal Basin, the great grain warehouses and River Craft Dock, the composite warehouses, the Graving Docks, cattle lairages, and the Tower Buildings, with their powerful engines and machinery and other sheds around the quays. As well there were the coal hoists and their several groups of railways, the Birkenhead, Woodside landing stage and floating roadway, the Wallasey landing stage and numerous other works.

On the Liverpool side of the River Mersey a vast amount of work was carried out for the development and improvement of the estate, including the north docks opened in 1881 by the Prince and Princess of Wales. They were the Huskisson Branch Dock and the alteration and part reconstruction of the Canada and Huskisson Docks, a new half-tide dock on the site of the Sandon Basin and the Wellington Half-tide Dock together with large entrances and deep sills to make them suitable for the largest and heaviest draft ships likely to come into use at that time. In many cases, this would be a lifetime's work for any engineer but not for George Lyster whose energy and devotion to his work was boundless.

This could be seen by the work carried out in the vicinity of the Pierhead, Waterloo Dock, with its large range of grain warehouses, many of which have disappeared with the progress of time, and West Waterloo Dock, the Prince's Half-tide Dock and river entrances, The combined landing stages and floating roadway on the site of St. George's Basin, the roadways leading to the stage, passenger sheds and customs accommodation and the south docks with their improved sheds and novel roof cranes.

On his arrival there was a total water area in the Liverpool and Birkenhead docks of 334 acres, and a quayage of 20 miles. On his retirement this had been increased to a water area of 531 acres and a quayage of 34 miles respectively. George Fosbery Lyster died in 1899.

7

Agnes Elizabeth Jones

---'We entertain angels unaware'

'The Londonderry Sentinal' 1868

When you tread the steps down into the Lady Chapel of Liverpool's most beautiful, gothic Anglican Cathedral, you will see the face of an angel looking down on you. On a bright day with the light shining through the window, the face of Agnes Jones lights up and her eyes meet your gaze you may feel she is looking into your inner thoughts.

Agnes Elizabeth Jones was born in Cambridge, November 10th, 1832. Her father was a Lieutenant Colonel, of the 12th Regiment, having been ordered there a few days previously. Agnes was a delicate child until she was nearly two years of age when she was taken to Ireland, the home of her grandparents and the birthplace of both her parents. Her father was born in Kildare 1795, and her mother, formerly Elizabeth Smyth, was born at Ardmore Derry. Agnes spent part of her early childhood at Ardmore and later, the family settled at Fahan House on the banks of Lough Swilly. On the 12th of August 1837 the Jones family sailed with their father's regiment from Cork for Mauritius, spending six years there. In 1843 after her father's health broke down, they returned home to Fahan House, a small but lovely spot on the banks of Lough Swilly, Co. Donegal.

From an early age Agnes had become involved with the welfare of others less fortunate than herself. In particular the care of the elderly, the poor and sick people at Fahan. The area described by one of the Jones family was of a heaven of natural beauty loved by Agnes.

We all became attached to this sweet home, but Agnes, especially, ever clung to it with the deepest affection. It lies nestled among trees at the foot of wild heath covered hills, the waters of the blue lake rippling up to the edge of the lawn and then stretching out to the grey hills at the other side. Every variety of scenery is combined in the little nook, bare rocky mountains which seem to bid defiance to the advance of cultivation, subsiding at their base into sunny fields or soft stretches of waving flax. Wooded park-like domains and bleak stony patches, alternating on the banks of the lovely lough, so appropriately called 'The Lake of Shadows' while here and there the blue smoke rises from isolated cottages which dot the landscape all along the winding shore.

In January 1848 Agnes and her sister were sent to the Miss Ainsworths' School, at Avonbank, Stratford-on-Avon. The two sisters had suffered under the severity of their governess and were hoping for a more pleasant change in their new environment. Their new place of learning was a cheerful and admirably managed school.

Commenting on Agnes, her sister Josephine wrote:

Her ardent affectionate nature was drawn out in warmest love to Miss Harriet Ainsworth, who perhaps never realized all the gratitude she had called forth in the enthusiastic young Irish girl, who now, for the first time, felt her powers brought into action and her efforts to please appreciated.

After two years and three months at the school Agnes and her sister returned to Ireland, on the death of their father on 19th March 1850. During the summer of that year, the family left their home at Fahan House for Dublin. Before leaving, Agnes and her sister met two ladies, a Miss Bellingham and Miss Mason who were engaged in missionary work among the Roman Catholics. In the summer of 1852 Agnes and her sister, together with two of her aunts, made a tour of Connemara and were excited by the scenery of the west. Agnes, was moved by the poor people of the area to such an extent, her sister Josephine wrote:

> Her heart was drawn in ardent love to the poor but intelligent peasantry, many of whom are wholly ignorant of the English language and all of whom had been brought up in utter ignorance of the truth as it is in Jesus. We visited many of the schools and as the Bishop of Tuam, with a large body of clergy, was making a Confirmation tour at the time, we heard several examinations of the bright-faced children in the schools, whose answers astonished and delighted us.
>
> The orphan nursery at Ballyconree especially interested Agnes and meeting her kind friends Miss Bellingham, and then Mrs. D'Arcy, the wife of the rector of Clifden and Miss Gore, was an additional pleasure. She would willingly have stayed behind us in the west to work for God with Miss Gore at Ballyconree, in that great field so wonderfully opened up for the labourer but duty called her away. It did seem as if her life-long desire for missionary work might some day find its realization in that sphere. She chose one school, which seemed in special need and for some years collected funds for the payment of the master. So

brightly did she picture the delights of Connemara that a friend gave her the name of "the recluse of Clare Island" and often playfully asked her when she intended to migrate to the wilds of the far west.

In 1853, at the age of twenty-one, Agnes spent some time with her sister and other members of her family in Bonn, Germany. She visited the Institution of Kaiserswerth, visiting hospitals and schools. Agnes with one of her aunts, spent a week at the Institution, and considered the training could be of use in Ireland. During this time Agnes was also influenced by the work of Florence Nightingale in the Crimea. In 1859 Agnes took herself off to London and was introduced to Florence at St. Thomas' Hospital and they became good friends.

Agnes entered St. Thomas' Hospital in October 1862, as a Nightingale student nurse. Later she was to spend a term as superintendent of a small hospital in London. This was later to be followed by her appointment as superintendent of the Great Northern Hospital London, during the years 1863-1864. Unknown to Agnes, at that time Mr. William Rathbone, a wealthy Liverpool merchant approached the Select Vestry of the Liverpool, Brownlow Hill Workhouse, and offered to put a trained nurse in the workhouse to replace the system of having the sick nursed by infirm female paupers. He said he would pay all the expenses of the new system for three years. The offer was accepted.

In August 1864, Agnes was requested to go to Liverpool to meet the committee and give her opinion on various debated points relative to the arrangements to be made for her staff. After the lonely journey from London, a carriage was waiting to drive Agnes from the station to the workhouse. The large black gates were opened and a man was waiting to conduct her to the Governor's house. After a long business interview she was shown the rooms she was eventually to occupy on the ground floor. The rooms looked out on a small court and low wall and beyond this lay the fever hospital. The rooms were dingy, furnished with a horsehair sofa, chairs, tables and a stool but no ornaments of any kind. The dark colour of walls gave a look of gloom to the whole interior. Undaunted, she went with the governor to visit the rooms proposed for her nurses and also visited the wards, later commenting on the latter:

The beds are rather close together and the wards low but all appeared fairly ventilated. There seemed care for the patients too plus a few plants and flowers, 'Illustrated News' pictures on the walls and a "silent comforter" in each ward, not the utterly desolate look one often meets in such places. I feel at this moment, completely at home here and the nervous fear I had in looking forward to it all, seems to have left me. I went to bed very happy and with the kind of feeling that I had indeed adopted the work. Whatever doubts I might have had before, seeing the place had made me feel I shall love it and be of some use. I trust, if God blesses and helps me to be of use to some of those poor lonely ones. I was awaiting them when Mrs. Cropper, senior and Mrs. J. Brougham came in, bringing a basket of lovely flowers all arranged in a glass vase, only needing water. It gave such a homelike look to my room and the kind thoughtfulness of the gift made me feel again the good hand of my God upon me. They soon left and I had a long time to wait, so I sat down to read the Bible alone and engrossed my mind, so ready to dwell on the nervous dread of the next hour. The ordeal was passed and no small weight removed from my mind by getting the first interview over. I remained for two more days so as to become perfectly acquainted with the proposed arrangements and suggest a few alterations. I asked myself, shall I ever be able to meet the dreariness, the loneliness, the difficulties, jealousies, restraint, disappointments, isolation? In my own strength, no never and yet when I look back, I see how God has helped me, how in the darkest moment something has come, sent by that loving Father, a little word, a letter, flowers, a something which has cheered me and told not only of the human love, but of that watchful heavenly Friend Who knew His weak child's need and answered her repining or fearing thought, by a message of mercy which bade her trust and not be afraid. I have many things to think of and plan. I fear the nurses having too much leisure. I know they cannot rightly employ it as a rule. Perhaps, with uneducated minds, too little is worse than too much work, responsibility too, weighs less on them. I am so glad I have been in the house, in everything I can now more realize my future position and its difficulties. But I have, as never before, a consciousness of power to bring sunshine to those poor creatures, as if I could, with God's blessing, make a little ray of hope and comfort sometimes enter their sad hearts.

Agnes returned to Liverpool in the spring of 1865 to take up her new post of Lady Superintendent. On her arrival, in order to brighten up her rooms and give a homelike comfort and elegance to them, Mr. and Mrs. W. Rathbone and members of the Cropper family filled them with various articles of furniture. Agnes felt overwhelmed by the kindness and gifts from the Rathbone and Cropper families and so touched by such kindness, Agnes recorded in her journal:

I was so humbled I could have sunk to the earth, I suppose the feeling is partly pride, the extreme dislike and sensitiveness I have to any obligation. But all this makes me feel as if people expected so much of me, this repaying beforehand of what I am expected to be and to do and to which I may never attain. Supposing, what is quite possible, I turn out incapable of conducting the scheme and have to be replaced not for any fault, but merely for want of the necessary governing and organizing power. I shall feel like the originator of the South Sea Bubble, for allowing people to be deluded by false expectations. I should equally dislike any future testimonial, but I could bear it more patiently had I been at work and done something. I shall look round on my furniture as if each thing were an accusing ghost.

I now spend about three hours daily going on my rounds of the wards, which does not give me long on each and as I have not yet assumed the reins, I cannot do anything, not even sit down to read to a patient. But I get a few words to most and I think already, many look for me. There is so much, that is very sad, which one realizes more when inactive in the way of remedy, but I hope we shall be able to lessen many evils in time, slowly and gradually it must be.

I hear few complaints and have very few requests, these chiefly for paper and stamps to write to friends and I receive many respectful nods from my countrymen. There is one very large ward entirely of Roman Catholics and on my first visit I had so many questions to answer, 'are you a Catholic?' etc. etc., as no other visitors are admitted. I see many in various directions, reading their Bibles and have met several who seem indeed to rejoice in them.

One bright little child especially, who is one mass of sores, always looks so happy and his large eyes dance with delight as he repeats hymns, etc. He speaks so imperfectly that I cannot ask him much, indeed my deafness makes me lose a great deal. There are many poor blacks here, one has died since I came, severe colds are so fatal to them. One man from Manila is dying and only one of the patients can understand his language. There are many idiots and old people in their dotage, one keeps a birch rod under his pillow which he daily presents to me, with a long speech, others cry if spoken to kindly. I feel daily more and more glad of the work in prospect, it is such a field of usefulness if God could only Bless us in it and I feel He will.

Few have had such a happy life as I have and it is happier every year. Today in one ward, lay a poor black man, the dews of death were on his face and his poor parched lips and gasping breath told the same tale. Oh! how, I longed to go and nurse him. I was able to say a few words to him of Jesus. He said he was so weak, but I told him how Jesus could tell the secret of the heart and accept the weakest longing. Oh! the loneliness of these sick beds. Oh! the many, many wants. How we shall need strength and hope and faith in God! Then the thought which every one repeats, that 'nobody ever comes into a place like this but by their own fault', meaning idleness or sin. A hospital is sad enough, but a workhouse! It almost seems as if over so many of those beds, 'no hope' must be written, with reference to this world, friendless and hopeless. If in this life only ye have hope, ye are all men most miserable. How we shall need the love of Christ to constrain us in our work, to be as He would have us be with those poor sufferers, not as man would have us! Today I was only in the medical wards. A Frenchman, who does not speak English, much enjoyed a talk. He so brightened up and made me such a French salute as I moved on. I gave him paper for writing and he seemed quite joyous with the thought of the answer.

An Italian was much cheered by my telling him I knew Naples well. I was rather horror-struck to hear that a policeman goes every night through the wards to keep order.

The feeling remained, of the class of insubordinates one would have to control. How earnestly I desire they may be the better of our coming here! Six hundred patients dependent for comfort, on my staff and me!

During this interval of waiting for the beginning of her work and the arrival of her trained nurses, Agnes wrote to Mrs. Pennefather on May 11 1865.

Dearest Mrs. Pennefather
I sit down to answer yours at once, as I have time

now which I may not have again for weeks, we have not yet begun. I have been living here nearly a month, but have weekly put off my staff, their rooms not being ready. We hope decidedly to begin on the 16th. I go daily to the wards to see the poor patients and I am on the spot when wanted about arrangements, this and preparing a lending library, is the extent of my work at present. I do not feel the time lost. I feel quite at home here now and am pretty much so in the wards, though not able to do anything, not being in office yet. It is more trying work, however, than if I felt something were doing. I see so much that needs a remedy and can only sometimes give a little hint how to make a sufferer easier, or do it myself. But the scenes of various kinds and many deaths are very sad and I feel very much the absolute prohibition to say a word to the Roman Catholics. My question about the separate wards for Protestants and Roman Catholics has been decided for me. One of the guardians, whom I asked, thought it would involve endless difficulties. Thank you so much for wishing to help me in it. I look often to you, on many points it seems as if I could ask no one else and your letters always help me so much, if only by their sympathy. It often seems strange that I, who have so little self-reliance and would like every step directed, am obliged to take such an independent position. And yet I have been so led on that I could not help it and I only trust I may be more and more led to look to the guidance of the Ever-present and All-wise Heavenly Friend. I really must apologize for this letter. I have written on, often interrupted and forgetting what I had said and so it has grown. My only excuse must be my deep feeling of longing for more labourers and wiser and better ones. I so deeply feel how few get training for that work which, of all work, needs it.

Agnes began work on the 18th of May 1865 as the first trained nurse in any public institution in Liverpool.

Brownlow Hill Workhouse was one of the biggest in the country, at times with over 3,500 people. In 1802 a fever hospital was built separate from the main body of the workhouse, because of the risk of contagious diseases (it was bigger than all the other Liverpool hospitals put together). At that time infectious disease was one of the great dangers in the workhouse community. On the 4th February 1867, Agnes wrote:

> I sometimes wonder if there is a worse place on earth, but I never regret coming and I never wish to give it up.

Less than two years after beginning her work, the new nursing system that she devised, was extended to the whole infirmary as a permanent arrangement, and her methods accepted by the rest of the country. Brownlow Hill Workhouse Hospital gradually ceased to be a place where the poor died without care, and in misery. Agnes fell ill on the 6th February 1868 and was found to be suffering from typhus fever. During the short illness, Florence Nightingale wrote to an aunt of Agnes. "I look on hers as one of the most valuable lives in England in the present state of the poor law and workhouse nursing". However Agnes never recovered from the fever and died in the early morning of 19th February 1868, at the early age of thirty-six.

The remains of Agnes Jones were taken back to Ireland, where her funeral took place at Fahan Co. Donegal, a few miles from Derry City. She was buried in the family tomb in Fahan Churchyard to rest in the land she loved so well.

In June of that year, Florence Nightingale wrote:

> One woman has died, a woman, attractive and rich, and young and witty; yet a veiled and silent woman. Distinguished by no other genius but the divine genius working hard to train herself in order to train others to walk in the footsteps of Him who went about

doing good. She died as she had lived, at her post, in one of the largest workhouse infirmaries in the kingdom. In less then three years she had reduced one of the most disorderly hospital populations in the world to something like Christian discipline such as the police themselves wondered at. She had disarmed all opposition and all sectarian zealotism; so that Roman Catholic and Unitarian, High Church, and Low Church all literally rose up and called her blessed.

William Rathbone erected a ten-foot high memorial to Agnes in the Liverpool workhouse with inscriptions composed by Florence Nightingale and Bishop William Alexander of Derry. It was in the form of an Angel in white marble standing on a stone plinth, named 'The Angel of the Resurrection'. The memorial was the work of the great Italian sculptor Pietro Tenerani 1789-1869. who studied with both Canova and Thorvaldsen, two of the early masters of Italian Sculpture. Of his many works on classical and Christian subjects, the best include 'Psyche with Pandora's Box', 'Cupid and Venus', and 'Deposition from the Cross' a large relief in the Lateran, Rome. He made the tomb of Pius VIII in St. Peter's Rome and a statue of Simon Bolivar, President of Colombia. When the Workhouse was finally demolished, the memorial was moved to Walton Hospital, in Liverpool. In 1989, it was again moved to the Oratory at Liverpool's Anglican Cathedral.

Liverpool's Anglican Cathedral also perpetuates her memory in 'The Noble Woman of the Staircase Window' in the Lady Chapel.

On November 13th 1932 a thanksgiving service was held at Liverpool Anglican Cathedral for the centenary commemorating two outstanding Irish Nurses, Catherine (Kitty) Wilkinson and Agnes Jones. Catherine Wilkinson came to prominence during the outbreak of cholera in Liverpool in 1832 and it was the centenary of the birth of Agnes in 1832. Nurses from London and other parts of the country attended the service, which was held in the nature of a national thanksgiving service. The work of the two women was seen to have been of great importance. William Rathbone was also identified with this and was instrumental in bringing Nurse Agnes Jones to Liverpool.

The people of Donegal and Derry held an Ecumenical service on the centenary of her burial, with an ecumenical service, attended by the Church of Ireland and Roman Catholic Bishops of Derry, and the Presbyterian and Methodist Church Leaders. There were many doctors and nurses present at Fahan Churchyard for the open-air commemoration in 1968.

Since 1869 a lasting memorial, a tablet of Carrara marble, entitled 'Grief' in memory of Agnes Jones, is displayed in the chancel of the Church of Ireland, Fahan, Co. Donegal. Robert Kell, Derry, delivered this piece, Bishop William Alexander of Derry and the people of Fahan commissioned it. On the base of the monument is a tribute from the Bishop William Alexander of Derry.

Alone with Christ in this sequestered place,
Thy Sweet Soul learn'd its quietude of grace,
On sufferers waiting in this vale of ours,
Thy gifted hand was trained to finer powers,
Therefore, when Death, O Agnes! came to thee-!
Not in the cool breath of our Silver sea,
But in the city hospitals' hot ward,
A gentle worker for the gentle Lord,
Proudly as men heroic ashes claim,
We ask'd to have thy fever stricken frame,
And lay it in our grass, beside our foam,
Till Christ the Healer calls His healers home.

Her sister Josephine in 'The memorials of Agnes Elizabeth Jones' gives a good description of the work of Agnes:

I believe that in Liverpool Workhouse Hospital, things were better managed than in any similar

66

institutions. An active governor and efficient committee prevented wholesale starvation or cruelty. But no general inspection can secure against individual oppression where the old system of pauper nursing prevails. Mr. W Rathbone proposed at once to substitute for those ignorant and worse than useless women, trained paid nurses and nobly undertook to bear all the expense connected with the experiment for three years. By which time he believed the success of the scheme would have recommended it to the board of guardians and it would be adopted as the permanent system. As soon as he obtained the consent of the committee, he wrote to my sister, who was then, in the spring of 1864, at the Great Northern Hospital, asking her to undertake the post of lady superintendent of the proposed trained nurses. After much correspondence with Miss Nightingale and Mrs. Wardroper on the subject, she agreed to this proposal. The plan could not, however, be commenced for several months; many alterations were necessary to secure proper accommodation for the staff and the nurses themselves had to be found. Miss Nightingale, who entered most warmly into the project, arranged that twelve of the Nightingale Nurses trained at St. Thomas's Hospital be sent to Liverpool. No materials exist, either in letters or memoranda, which will allow me to give a history of the work, which Agnes attempted and accomplished in the Liverpool Workhouse. Her life there was too busy a one to allow time for much writing and her home letters dwelt on the little details which she knew would interest us and gave no idea of the greatness of her undertaking, or her plan of operation. The hope, therefore, entertained by those who, originally suggested the idea of this memoir, that some history of the results of her work, some suggestions as to the way in which it was conducted, some idea of the general organization might be obtained which would serve as a help to others treading in the same path, must be renounced.

That she thought over the subject and formed very decided opinions as to the relative merits of different organizations and administrations, we know, but she never had time to express these on paper.

Her letters and her diary, both hastily written (for time was very precious during those three last years) gave no idea of the immense work she organized, or of her practical ability and great business powers. It has even been thought and suggested, by one of those whose opinion I have great respect, that the deficiency which must arise because of this, is a reason why this memoir should not be published and that it will tend to lower the vague but yet high appreciation, which does exist in the minds of many, as to what she accomplished in the Liverpool Workhouse?

I trust that the existence of her work, recognized by all who take an interest in the subject of workhouse nursing, will obviate this danger. The memoir has been compiled, not for the benefit of poor-law boards and Boards of Guardians, but for Christian women, who, reading the story of her consistent walk in paths of no ordinary difficulty and moved by the example of unwavering devotion to her Heavenly Master's work, may go and do likewise.

On the 16th of June 2000 'Ireland's Own' published the story of Agnes Elizabeth Jones, an Irish pioneering nurse. After reading the story, Mary Devlin and her sister Margaret McGrath, from Fahan Co. Donegal set about finding the resting-place of this pioneering nurse at Fahan churchyard. Margaret and Mary found the family tomb including Agnes covered in vegetation and the surrounding railings in a sorry state covered in rust. They promptly set about clearing the area to give a better view of the tomb and a metal plaque bearing the name of Agnes Elizabeth Jones. The Devlin sisters represent The Inishowen Heritage Trust, and Fr. Edward Doherty, owner of Fahan House, since 1982, previous home of Agnes Jones, is President, of the Trust. The Inishowen

Trust is now setting up a memorial to Agnes Elizabeth Jones and having her grave as a focal point of remembrance. Not content with finding the resting-place of Agnes, the Devlin sisters, then set out for Liverpool where Agnes Jones put into practice her nursing skills on behalf of the poor of the town. Within a few days of arriving in Liverpool they had spread their net far and wide like good fishermen, to pull in some wonderful people to help them in their quest. They visited the Catholic Metropolitan Cathedral that stands on the site where Agnes carried out her good work with the assistance of other nurses whom she had taken with her to the Liverpool Workhouse Hospital. They also visited the Anglican Liverpool Cathedral to see the tribute is paid to Agnes in the 'Ladies of the Staircase Window' in the Lady Chapel of Liverpool Cathedral. One of the highlights of the visit, was the 'Angel of the Resurrection'. The 'Inishowen Heritage Trust' aims to commission a bronze statue of Agnes Elizabeth Jones, to be placed in the grounds of Fahan House. "The Londonderry Sentinel" February 25, 1868 stated:

Such lives are like the rainbow in the clouds – the assurance of hope – the hope that, be the times what they may, kindness and self-devotion shall never perish from the earth.

Then how does this quiet every day life-work contrast with the noisy flaunting zeal which characterizes some of our efforts. No parade. No show to call attention to her work. Simply the patient, unswerving performance of daily duty. Some of the noblest workers the world has ever known have been the quietest; so quiet that the world has known nothing about them until it has reaped the fruit of their labours. As in the olden time so it is even now – we entertain Angels unaware, and know not that they have been with us until they are gone, and we mark the void that is left by their departure.

The former home of the Jones family, with the author standing in the foreground. Agnes spent part of her childhood in this house.

Agnes in the 'Ladies of the Staircase Window' in the Lady Chapel, Liverpool Anglican Cathedral

"The Angel' memorial to Agnes Jones in The Workshop Hospital before the building was destroyed in 1929. This is now in the Oratory at Liverpool's Anglican Cathedral.

Front of Workhouse Infirmary, Brownlow Hill

Back of Workhouse Infirmary, Brownlow Hill

8

Dr. John Bligh

---Dr. Bligh was a great student of the Irish language and literature. The subject is especially interesting, because Gaelic is one of the still living Celtic languages.

'Liverpool's Legion of Honour'

Dr. John Bligh, M.D., M.C., the younger brother of Dr. Alexander Murray Bligh was also a distinguished member of his profession. John Bligh was born on the 4th January 1840 at Castlehacket, Tuam, County Galway, He was educated at Queen's College, Galway, and was a graduate of Queen's University, Belfast. He held the first scholarship in medicine during the medical course, 1860 to 1865, and was the first to whom the degree of M.C. (Master in Surgery) of the Queen's University was granted. Some of his fellow students were Lord McDonnell, Sir Andrew Reed, Dr John Conway, T. P. O'Connor, Lord Atkinson and Sir William Thomson. Dr. John Bligh came to Liverpool as assistant to Dr. Parsons in 1862, when the training of a doctor consisted mainly in being apprenticed to another practitioner. John Bligh was married in 1876 to Frances Mary Harris, daughter of Frederick Harris and they had a daughter and two sons. Liverpool's Legion of Honour portrayed Dr. John Bligh, in 1893 in the following way:

Dr. John Bligh is in the prime of life. He has made his mark in Liverpool and was for six years a member of the City School Board, resigning on account of pressure of professional duties. Dr. Bligh was a great student of the Irish language and literature. The subject is especially interesting, because Gaelic is one of the still living Celtic languages. Dr. Bligh chats with the ardour of an enthusiast on this, to him, attractive theme. He will tell you how the oldest existing specimens of the Irish language are to be found in sepulchral inscriptions in Ireland, and in the glosses affixed to Latin words in documents transcribed by Irish monks.

Do you want to listen to an aria on the *Book of Armagh* or the *'Book of Hymns'*? Go to Dr. Bligh, and he will dilate on the ancient character of these Irish manuscripts, and, perchance, will give you quaint excerpts from the metrical Festologies of Aengus Ceile De, the Martyrlogy of Tallaght and of Marionus O'Gorman. Of very special interest to Dr Bligh are the mediaeval Irish manuscripts relating to medicine, with their quaint commentaries on the then known medical authors of Europe and the East. With such tastes Dr. Bligh may be excused for being something of a laudator (eulogizer) temporis acti (delivery).

John Bligh was a great lover of music. He was closely associated with Carl Rosa and leading members of his opera company. Amongst his singing friends were Barton McGuchin, Leslie Crotty and his wife Madam Georgina Burns, Maria Roze, Eugene Goosens. When Carl Rosa retired as director of his opera company he taught singing at 117 Mount Pleasant in Liverpool, the home of Dr John Bligh. 'The Liverpool Review' reported on the Abercromby Branch Irish National League, paying a tribute to Dr. John Bligh:

Honour to whom honour is due was the prevailing sentiment on Monday evening last at the Meyerbeer Hall, Hardman Street, when Dr. John Bligh, the most chivalrous and loveable of men, was presented by the members of the Abercromby Branch Irish National League and a few friends with a finely illuminated address and silver salver, as a slight recognition of his faithful services to the Irish national cause in Liverpool.

There was a crowded attendance of members and their friends, the chair being occupied by Mr. John

74

Hand, who had many influential supporters. Prominent among these was the eminent baritone, Mr. Leslie Crotty, who had, with commendable patriotism, attended the meeting to do honour to an esteemed fellow-townsman, both Messrs. Bligh and Crotty being natives of Galway.

Prior to the presentation, Miss Amanda Fabris, Miss Grace Digby, and Mr. Aynsley Cooke, of the Carl Rosa Opera Company, gave several vocal items 'sans reproche', Mr. Goosens presided at the piano. The address, was read by Mr. G. S. Kelly, the hon. secretary, as follows: Dear Dr. Bligh, We the members of the Abercromby Branch of the Irish National League, of which since its formation, now several years ago, you have been president and we are desirous of offering you our congratulations on the success which under your presidency the branch has achieved. We recognise that in you we have a president in whom we can place the utmost confidence, one generous without ostentation, self-sacrificing, devotedly patriotic, and possessing in a large degree that true nobility which is ever tolerant of the failings of others, one who, in a word, is a potent influence and determining factor in all that is good and useful in our councils, and who, by characteristic amiability and almost religious devotion to the cause of Ireland, has endeared himself to us all.

We desire to place this on record, and to say, as no strangers to your many estimable qualities, how deeply and truly we respect and esteem you. As a slight but sincere token of that respect and esteem, we, in conjunction with a few other friends, ask your acceptance of this address, and of the piece of plate, which accompanies it. They will, when the national struggle is over and Ireland's rights are conceded, serve as souvenirs of the contest in which we were on behalf of dear old Ireland, and in which under your guidance the Abercromby Branch endeavoured to perform its part. Wishing you every blessing, we are, dear Dr. Bligh, your friend and fellow worker in the national cause.

Dr. Bligh in response said, 'That while I do not admit being worthy of such handsome gifts, they came from the spontaneous action of honest hearts'. He said he could not feel sufficiently thankful to those present for such kindly tokens of respect. With regard to his work in the cause of Ireland, he said, he had always felt that the love of country and of race was the love of life itself, and every true patriot must take to heart the maxim non sibi sed patrice. If they did this they would one day find, in the words of the address, 'the national struggle over, and Ireland's rights conceded'. When I came to Liverpool said Dr Bligh, 'the Irish people of this city were in a very obscure position, and exercised little influence'.

In 1879 it is almost certain that John and his brother Alexander would have celebrated the centenary celebration of the birth of Irish poet Tom Moore, who was born on the 28th of May 1779. The Liverpool Irish were rapidly adding their own culture to this great city. Throughout time the Irish people had embraced a love of poetry long before the written word. 'The Liberal Review' recognised this when on May 31, 1879 when they paid a tribute to Tom Moore:

Centenaries and celebrations of the memories of great men, such as Spinosa, the greatest of modern Jews, Voltaire, Goethe, Shiller, and Scotland has done the same with Scott and Burns, last month, we celebrated the anniversary of Shakespeare's 315th birth. This week Tom Moore has come in. The proceedings of the celebration and centenary of the birth of the brilliant Irishman were characterised by immense enthusiasm in Dublin, in Liverpool and other towns. In Liverpool there was a happy mixture of nationalities, as there always should be when we celebrate a poet, and of all religions, too, as still more there should be on such an occasion, for poetry, while it is the language of the universal religion, disdains to be shut up within the limits of a creed. Tom Moore deserves the praises bestowed on him in the eloquent oration of Mr. A. M. Sullivan.

Not the least among his claims to grateful remembrance is the fidelity with which he clung to the Roman Catholic faith at a time when Roman Catholics were still suffering under penal laws and men sacrificed their conscience daily for the sake of comfort and to promote the sacred gospel of getting on. It was the custom of the Catholic Irishmen to declare themselves Protestants in order to enter Trinity College and to intend to declare themselves Catholic again when their college career was finished. Of course, the result of this custom in multitudes of cases was sheer religious indifference.

Moore's parents debated whether their son should run the risk. Fortunately, they were not called to decide. For Trinity College was opened to Roman Catholics in the year when it was desirable for him to enter and thus he was able to secure a university education without having to pay for it the terrible price of denying his faith. All through his life Moore was a devout and intelligent Roman Catholic of the old school and he is represented much more faithfully by men like Dr. Dollinger, than by the modern ultramontane (faction within the Roman Catholic Church).

For our part, we pay our need of honour to men of all creeds so long as they know the reasons why they hold them and are superior to selfish ends. Moore's patriotism was equally honest and thorough with his religious fidelity. He would not barter his soul, or what he conceived to be his religious obligations, for the smiles of fortune. He was open to argument and open to conviction, but was proof against temptation and turned a deaf ear to the wiles of worldly Churchmen. He lived long enough to secure the good opinion of men who differed entirely from him in his religious conclusions and who would have scorned him and justly scorned him, had he pretended to be a Protestant.

In his early days Ireland was politically as well as religiously oppressed. He devoted himself manfully to her service and laboured to win for her the measure of justice and equality to which she had a right and of which she has received large instalments during the present generation. He in the best Whig circles in London and did a great deal to create and to keep alive the interest in Irish politics which as borne abundant fruit in later times. Even the plots of the period were not outside his sympathies.

At Trinity College he was captivated by Robert Emmett and but for the watchful care of his mother, might have been involved in the sad catastrophe, which over took that ill-fated genius. As it was, he sang Emmett's praises in the Irish melodies. He set the woes of Ireland to touching music in beautiful verse, so that sympathy with them became fashionable in drawing rooms and people who were proof against hard facts put in plain prose were somehow mystically persuaded by the poet. In this way Moore may claim with O'Connell the right to be still the Liberator.

Moore's poetry is sweet rather than strong, clear rather than profound, bewitching and persuasive in its tenderness rather than carrying us away by grand and fiery passion. Compare 'Lallah Rookh' with 'Childe Harold'? Now, it is decidedly in the former poem that we see Moore at his very best as a poet. But in one canto of 'Childe Harold' there is more of the divine afflatus than in all that he ever wrote. Indeed among the galaxy of the stars that shone in the early part of the century, Ireland has every reason to cherish Moore's memory.

Tom Moore was a true poet, though of minor ideas. He was a fresh hearted, patriotic and thoroughly straightforward Irishman who stood true to his country. He was simply and naturally religious and though he wrote himself down a Roman Catholic, there was no narrowness and no bigotry in him. The Catholicity was the essence of his nature and the Romanism was the offspring of his birth and education. He deserved a centenary celebration. He was born 100 years ago on the 28th of May 1779.

It was known that when Dr. John Bligh first set foot in Liverpool, he felt that the Irish people in the town were in a very obscure position. "Only two men can be said to have had any appreciable influence and they were Mr. Michael James Whitty, of the 'Daily Post', an excellent and fluent orator, and Mr. John Yates." He had an admiration and friendship with Charles Stewart Parnell,

Dr John Bligh died March 8th 1913 aged seventy-three at his home in 117 Mount Pleasant, Liverpool, and a Requiem Mass took place at St. Nicholas Copperas Hill. The funeral took place at SS Peter and Paul, Great Crosby.

The principal mourners were Dr. J. P. Bligh, Mr. J. A. Bligh and Mr. M. M. Bligh (sons) Dr. Murray Bligh (nephew), Mrs. Murray Bligh, Mr. Thomas McEvoy (nephew) Mr. and Mrs. E. H. Hobby (brother-in-law) and sister. Frs. Cole, O'Connell and Casey, Mr. Massey Lynch, Fr. Walsh, Dr. Allen, Mr. T. Rudden Dr. Buchanan, Frs. Ryan, Crook, Bamber, McGrath and Norris. Dr. Alexander Bligh, Shaw Sreet, owing to illness was unable to attend his brother's funeral.

Amongst the general body of mourners were Alderman Taggart, Alderman Purcell, Mr. W. J. Burgess J.P., Colonel W. Walker J.P., Mr. J. P. Kelly (Liverpool and District Committee United Irish league), Mr. W. F. Ellis (Liverpool Young Ireland Society), Messrs. E. Horrigan and R. Philbin (Select Vestry), Mrs. Lynch (Convent of the Cenacle, New Brighton), Mr. P. Maguire (H.M. Customs)

Councillors, F. J. Harford J.P., Austin Harford J.P., Joseph Hughes, J. Bolger, John Clancey, Mr. E. Doran,

(St. Peters Guild), Rev. Bro. O'Shea (Catholic Institute). The Rev. J. North (Litherland), Fr. Commaleach, Fr. Smythe, Fr. J. Ross, Fr. Green (Bootle), Fr. Blanchard (St. Charles), Mr. F. Burke (Rock Ferry). Dr. McCormack, Mr. H. Peet J.P., Dr. J. P. Martin, Mr. C. O'Beirne, Dr. Rushton Parker, Mr. P. T. Daly, Dr. O'Sulivan, Mr. J. Falkner, Mr. J. S. Rimmer, Dr. F. H. Barendt, Dr. W. Alexander, Dr. W. A. MacMahon Garry, Mr. J. H. Wood, Dr. Bickerton, Messer Justin Lynskey, Hugh McAleavey. Eter Scott, junr, Dr. Cummins, Messrs L. Marr, F. O'Neill, H. W. French, W. H. Redmond, D. J. Clarke, M. O'Mahoney, J. McDonald, M. Flanagan, J. Allen, E. Rourke, H. Flynn, Dr. C. H. Hughes, Messrs J. Martin, H. C. Quinn, T. P. Maguire, J. Bird, E. H. Morton, P. S. Bullen

Among the many mourners of the deceased was his son, Dr John Patrick Bligh and nephew Dr. John Murray Bligh, Alderman Taggert, Alderman Purcell, M. W. Burgess, J.P., Colonel William Walker J. P. Mr. J. P. Kelly (Liverpool and District Committee, United Irish League) W.F. Ellis (Liverpool Young Ireland Society), Councillors F.T. Harford J.P. Austin Harford J.P.

'The Liverpool Daily Post', 9th March 1913.

9

Alderman
Dr. Alexander Murray Bligh

---Of what greater importance to a populace, he aptly asks, than whether they have fresh air, pure water, good drainage, unadulterated food and open space for exercise?

'Liverpool's Legion of Honour'

In the 1860s Liverpool was blessed with the arrival of Dr. Alexander Murray Bligh who was born in 1838 at Castle Hackett, Tuam, Galway. He served his adopted town both in politics and medicine, and then he became a town councillor for one of the Vauxhall Wards in 1871. 'Liverpool's Legion of Honour' portrayed Alexander Murray Bligh, in 1893, in the following way:

Alexander Murray Bligh has rendered long and yeoman service on the City Council, to which he was first elected twenty-one years ago. He is a medico. He was educated at St. Jarlath's College, Tuam, at Queen's College, Galway and finally at the Dublin Medical Schools. He married Mary Agnes Elizabeth Brady, of Kenilworth Square, Rathgar, Dublin.

In politics Mr. Bligh is a Nationalist. He favours the creation of an Irish Parliament to sit in Dublin and to have power to legislate on and to regulate Irish affairs. He argues that the Union has brought neither loyalty, peace nor strength. The attempt on the part of England to govern Ireland according to English ideas has been, he considers, a disastrous failure. He points to the fact that the old Irish Parliament, although returned by a corrupt and limited electorate, did a vast amount of useful work and a successor constructed on better lines and sounder principles would be, he thinks, eminently efficient.

Mr. Bligh, during his nearly quarter of a century experience of City Council work, has laid special emphasis on the importance of sanitary science. 'Sanitas Sanitatum, omnia sanitas' has been his watchword. He has laudably aimed at securing conditions of life worthy of a city of 'Hygiene'. He will tell you that there are two obstacles, which the advocates of sanitary reform have to combat – a general dislike of centralisation and the popular dread of taxation. He shares the wholesome British prejudice against over government. He knows that it is always emasculating and is some times even demoralising. Centralisation may, of course, be beneficially employed, as when it is used to systematise, stimulate and strengthen local authorities. The same may be said with regard to taxation. Over taxation is bad, but who can object to reasonable imposts, levied for securing the people the essentials of a healthy existence?

Even now, as Mr. Bligh well argues, there is plenty of scope for the schoolmaster's efforts in educating the people in the value of good sanitation. Scientists may make discoveries, philanthropists may popularise them and municipal authorities may give them official recognition, but Mr. Bligh maintains these will be in vain if the people do not second their efforts. Of what greater importance to a populace, he aptly asks, than whether they have fresh air, pure water, good drainage, un-adulterated food and open space for exercise? Efficient sanitation has its patriotic as well as its hygienic bearing.

The inhabitants of back slums and crowded courts are feeble, rickety and stunted. They have about them all the signs of premature debility, degeneracy and decay. Their children inherit and perpetuate their shattered and enfeebled constitutions. How important then Mr. Bligh's contention, that if the English, Scottish and Irish are to hand down unimpaired their magnificent race traditions our sons must not only have stout and brave hearts, but athletic frames, which, he rightly insists, can only be obtained by a proper observance of the laws of health.

Mr. Bligh has held the position of Medical Advisor to the D. I. Board Schools and other scholastic institutions in the city and several Insurance Companies and in these and other capacities he has right worthily maintained the best traditions of the distinguished profession to which he belongs.

Alexander Murray Bligh was living in 59 Shaw Street at the time of his death, at the age of eighty-nine on the 18th April 1922. His wife Mary Agnes Bligh died aged, sixty-nine years, on the 6th May 1924.

Alexander Murray Bligh's son, John Murray Bligh, was also attracted to the medical profession. He was born the 1st January 1879 in Liverpool. He was educated at Castleknock College, Dublin, and Liverpool University College. In 1826, he married Elizabeth Emily Underwood and they had three sons. In 1902 he was the last president of the Student Representative Council before it became the Guild of Undergraduates of the new University. He was a house surgeon at the Liverpool Royal Infirmary in 1905 and later held junior posts at the Northern Hospital and the Infirmary for Children.

His earliest consultant appointment was as honorary assistant physician to the Liverpool Infirmary for Children, later incorporated into the Royal Liverpool Children's Hospital. For a time he held a similar position at Stanley Hospital. In 1916 he was elected honorary assistant physician at the David Lewis Northern Hospital, to which he became full physician in 1918. He served in The Royal Army Medical Corps in the First World War. He was with No. 12 Indian General Hospital, with the rank of captain. He was consulting physician to several voluntary hospitals and other charities including the Southport Infirmary, the Lourdes Hospital and Royal Liverpool Children's Hospital. He was also visiting physician to Belmont Road and Ormskirk County Hospitals.

His university posts were those of clinical lecturer in medicine and in diseases of children. He held several offices in the Liverpool Medical Institution and was elected president in 1934. He served as Justice of the Peace in Liverpool from 1938 to 1948. He enjoyed his retirement at Formby, near Liverpool, prior to his death at the age of ninety in 1948. 'The British Medical Journal' in its obituary notices read:

John Murray Bligh had the strong outlook of so many of the consultants of his time. He was a general physician with a special interest in paediatrics. For him medicine was practised first and foremost at the bedside. He was a man of high principles and absolute integrity, loyal to his hospital and to his friends. He was gifted with a natural charm and dignity, and the classical education of an earlier generation gave distinction to his speech and writings. He was proud of his Irish decent, and like so many of his fellow countrymen was a very entertaining raconteur. As a sportsman he was an enthusiastic angler, and preferred the Irish rivers to all others. To his wife and three sons we offer our sincere sympathy.

10

Councillor Patrick Byrne

--Patrick, you were the first and best champion these poor ever had. You voted for Sunday opening of the Gallery and Museum.
                                              'Liverpool Citizen' newspaper.

Of all the wonderful characters portrayed, in this volume Patrick Byrne is one the most colourful. In 1863, aged seventeen, he arrived in Liverpool from Ireland with empty pockets and only the clothes that covered the large-limbed young man over six-foot tall.

Patrick Byrne was born in 1845, in the Townland of Tinneshrule in the Parish of Ferns, County Wexford. Ferns is probably the most unaltered village in Ireland and Patrick would still be able to recognize it today except for the modern mode of transport. The village is situated on the N11, between the market towns of Gorey and Enniscorthy and whichever way you turn its rich history holds you in its embrace. The Normans, who came to Ireland in 1169 at the request of Diarmuid MacMurrough, the deposed King of Leinster, left their mark with a castle, and another of their historic sites is Saint Aidans Cathedral. Almost fifty years before the birth of Patrick Byrne, Wexford and its people were to live through the tragic events of the rebellion of 1798. His parents would have held their infant son in their arms at the start of one of the saddest periods of Ireland's history, the Famine of 1845-51.

As a boy the Irish Board of Works employed him for some time. His hours were long as he laboured on farms, attending thatches, and helping stonemasons. His young head would have been filled with adventure and like so many young people before him, he decided to leave his homeland to sail for Liverpool in 1862-63. He settled in the Vauxhall area, which housed many who fled the Famine of 1847, and were still recovering from their ordeal.

Patrick soon found work as a dock labourer, working under conditions enforced by employers who cared little for the welfare of those in their employ, as labour was cheap and plentiful and he soon made many friends among the ranks of those who toiled alongside him. Patrick ceased to be a dock labourer after three years as Liverpool was a town of opportunity for a young man who had set his goals in life much higher than the toil of a long day on the docks. Almost every penny he earned he saved to open a small lodging house in the town and it was not long before he became the occupier of 'The Tichfield' a public house in Tichfield Street in the Vauxhall area.

Scotland Place showing the Morning Star Pub.

It was during the time that he was landlord of this establishment, that Patrick acquired the sobriquet of 'Dandy Pat'. He would often wear a sealskin coat with a vent and a white hat and although he was a very popular landlord, he was also a very shrewd businessman. He began to prosper with his boundless energy and in November 1876, at the age of thirty-one, he was able to acquire the 'Morning Star' a very large hotel in Scotland Place, Byrom Street. The hotel was in a bad state of repair but Patrick renovated it and the people flocked in. It was during this period that the Temperance League warned of the evils of alcohol.

Many in Liverpool, during the late nineteenth century, lived in some of the vilest conditions imaginable, houses in the courts lacked even the basic means that we expect today, such as running water. And so pubs such as the 'Morning Star' offered a warm environment during the short winter days. Drink was a business and the more a man could imbibe, the greater his welcome. Patrick felt people should be able to do more than just get drunk so he installed two billiard tables at a time when such recreation in licensed premises was unheard of. As proprietor of the 'Morning Star' he also organized tournaments, formed billiard teams and put up prizes. The 'Morning Star' was to become his flagship, and Patrick went on to acquire more property, including public houses in several parts of the city. He acquired 'The Rock Ferry Hotel', which at one time was a very fashionable establishment. Patrick also had under his control, it is said, a very well known hotel in Dale Street, the business centre of the town.

Patrick began to take an interest in politics in 1879 and he was associated with Dr. Cummins, Dr. John Bligh, Dr. Alexander Murray Bligh, Mr. Hugh Fox, Mr. William Madden, Mr. L Connolly and other leaders of the Irish Party. He took part in establishing the Liverpool branch of the Home Rule Association and was always to be found at the meetings, either as a speaker or a worker. The following year, 1880 the 'Liverpool Daily Post' reported:

He began to meddle in election affairs chiefly with an eye to business. His untimely obtrusion was one of the obstacles, which prevented the Liberal party securing the majority in the Town Council. The Council at the time of the November elections was equally divided and the turning point was the St. Anne's Ward election. There were two candidates, Dr. Cross (an Alderman), who was nominated by the Conservatives and Mr. T. S. Little, a Liberal. Little was a total abstainer, and was certain of the support of the teetotalers, a great number of whom were members of the Temperance League, which had been formed some time before by Father Nugent.

The other Irish electors in the Ward were expected to follow the lead of the Temperance Party, given the support of their parish priests. The return of Mr. Little was a matter of certainty and the Liberals would thus have a majority of one, by which they could return Liberal Aldermen instead of the retiring Tories. It was at this critical juncture that Patrick interposed in the interests of his trade.

He went about among his countrymen, with whom by this time he had become popular, and he contrived to divide them and draw a few of them away from voting for the Liberal candidate. When the poll closed the voting stood, Cross 1,070 Little 1,018—majority for the Conservatives, 52. This election was a turning point in the history of the Council and was also a new dimension in the career of Pat Byrne. His behavior gave great offence to the leaders of the Irish Party and thenceforth for some time there was so much antagonism between him and them that for the most part he took his own course. He began to develop a spirit of this kind even as early as February 1880, during the Whitley–Ramsey contest for the Parliamentary representation in Liverpool, when there was a difficulty in bringing the Irish party and the Liberals into line.

Pat Byrne was amongst those who seemed less

inclined to co-operate with the Liberal party and at some of the earlier meetings during the election, he assumed a prominent attitude of opposition. Those incidents, however, were passed over and Pat Byrne continued to interest himself in all the Irish movements, taking a prominent part in the work of the Land League and the National League and of the Ladies Land League for the relief of evicted tenants.

The meetings of those organizations at that period, 1881-1882 were held in a hall in Hatton Garden where Pat Byrne, Dr. Cummins, Mr. Garton, Dr. John Bligh, Dr. Alexander Murry Bligh and other gentlemen spoke, Sunday after Sunday, to crowded audiences. The League was driven to find more suitable premises and they began occupy a larger hall in Great Crosshall Street. Pat Byrne and Mr. Garton becoming sureties for the rent and they addressed meetings in support of the Land League.

Patrick first tried his hand at politics when a seat became vacant in the St. Peter's Ward in 1881 but it was to no avail as it was a safe Liberal seat. He was also defeated in 1882. But the death of Patrick De Lacy Garton, councillor for Scotland Ward, in 1883 gave Patrick Byrne the opportunity to try his hand at politics for the third time. He won the vacant seat on the 5th September with 1690 votes and wasted no time in representing his constituents. During the eight or nine weeks leading up to the municipal elections on the 9th of November of the same year Patrick became a thorn in the side of the Conservatives. 'The Liverpool Review' 11th August wrote:

A majority 539 has returned Mr. P. Byrne, who is principally known as a Scotland Road publican and an extreme Irish Nationalist, to the Liverpool City Council over his Conservative opponent and by a majority 1690 over the individual who came forward as a 'Labour candidate'. In the meantime the remarkable fact has to be accounted for the abstentions amounted to 4532, or nearly two-thirds of the constituency.

For some reason the vote went against him in November 1883, and Joseph Simpson won the seat with 1930 votes, while Patrick's was 1805. Byrne took no pains to disguise his feelings with regard to the Liberals and at the very first favourable opportunity was determined to enter the Council for the second time by ousting one of them. Pat did not have to wait long, as he opposed the re-election of Mr. C. McArdle for Vauxhall Ward in 1884. The fact that McArdle was a Nationalist cut no ice with Pat Byrne. He stood as a Home Ruler and pooled 652 votes, while McArdle who appeared before the ratepayers as a Liberal, which party he had represented since 1875, secured the support of only 423 votes.

From that date Pat Byrne sat for Vauxhall Ward without opposition. As a member of the Council, he always advocated what he considered to be in the interest of the working people of the town. He also took advantage of every possible occasion to ventilate the grievances of the Irish section of the ratepayers, especially in times of scarcity through want of work, and during severe winters. It frequently happened that the 'Morning Star Hotel' was turned into a sort of relieving house for the poor of the district. Whenever any charitable movement was inaugurated, Pat Byrne was certain to be found on the committee. One of those occasions was during the dock labourers' strike.

In the Council he also advocated the pensioning of old servants who had for years worked in humble capacities and he never tired of contrasting their cases with those of retiring well-paid officials. He frequently criticised the working of several committees. He constantly complained that the Health Committee was clearing away dwelling houses without providing others in their place, thus turning Scotland Ward and Vauxhall Ward into a desert and ruining the shopkeepers who were gradually finding themselves without customers.

Pat Byrne was especially critical of the Watch Committee. On one occasion he was grossly assaulted at a hall in Netherfield Road, which the Home Rulers had just opened. He bore the marks of the maltreatment upon his face and it was generally believed that he never fully recovered from the wounds inflicted upon his head, 'The Liverpool Review' wrote:

Patrick lived in the midst of the people and took care more than once to remind colleagues in the Council who treated his speeches with some amount of derision, that he knew what was desired better than men of great wealth and high position living in the comparative retirement of our parks or perhaps further afield, where the cry of suffering humanity was never heard. There was the true ring of sincerity about all he said, and how could more point be given to this assertion than by remembering the practical way he set about relieving poor people, at one period of the year at any rate, by the provision of Christmas cheer. Many a time had he undertaken the thankless task of harassing the powers that be, in the conduct of municipal affairs in order that some obscure widow of a street cleaner should receive the full allowance from the Corporation on the death of her husband.

However, it was not just the poor who benefited from the generosity of Patrick. He made a generous gift of new alabaster altar railings to Holy Cross Church. However 'The Liverpool Review' attacked his generosity:

Irishmen are proverbially reckless in their generosity and the public line of business is a more or less profitable one. But there was munificence about this gift, which showed a largeness of idea not usually associated with what was known of the character of mine host of the 'Morning Star' and other liquor palaces in the lower parts of the city. He had never given anyone reason to regard him as a philanthropist or a patron of religious art.

In April 1885 just six months after Patrick took his seat on the Council for the second time, a debate took place on the question of insanitary housing. Certain Conservative members, led by Mr. J. B. Smith, Mr. John Hughes, Alderman Jennings and Dr. Hamilton, were of the opinion that the insanitary dwellings in what was termed 'The Little Ireland', in the heart of Liverpool should be left alone. The Irish nationalists lead by Patrick Byrne, supported J. B. Smith and Company, but for very different reasons, to the Conservatives. Mr. J. B. Smith although Chairman of the Health Committee, made it known that the dwellings of the poor were of no concern to him, or to anybody else. He felt it was nobody's business to improve or demolish them however detrimental they were to the health of the community. Dr. Hamilton showed great hostility towards Dr. Taylor, the Medical Officer of Health, for supporting the removal of insanitary property, whilst Mr. John Hughes based his opposition on the alleged oppression and injustice suffered by owners of insanitary property.

Patrick Byrne regarded the removal of poor people from this type of property onto the street without a roof over their heads as 'eviction'. Large numbers of poor people had their houses demolished when no other shelter was available in the area. The plight of the homeless poor was regarded as a temporary inconvenience and the term 'eviction' a decided exaggeration. The Insanitary Property Committee did not accept responsibility for the plight of those left without shelter when the demolition of property that was impossible to improve became a sanitary necessity. The committee felt they were no more responsible for any hardship, than if the same places had accidentally burnt down, or had suddenly fallen into ruins. Mr. A. B. Forwood leader of the conservatives addressing the subject of the demolition gave his answer to the problem:

The dwellers in the insanitary 'Cave' and all others who doubt the work of the committee. By the end of the present year, some fifteen hundred of the most insanitary houses in the city would have been swept away and streets hitherto pestilent and fever stricken would be opened up into the broad and healthy thoroughfares. The Nash Grove dwellings would be occupied, accommodating 280 families, with front doors opening upon a playground. This is substantial progress and instead of criticising it in a spirit of aimless hostility the dwellers in the insanitary 'Cave' would do well to address themselves to the task of showing that it has been either precipitate or ill advised, or that it is, on economic grounds a financial mistake.

It was an open secret that Patrick was interested in gaining a seat in Parliament in the forth-coming Parliamentary Elections in November 1885. The Home Rulers proposed Patrick Byrne for the Liverpool seat, but Charles Stewart Parnell, leader of the Nationalist in Parliament, was determined that T. P. O'Connor should stand for the Scotland Division. O'Connor had been the member for Galway, but desired a more high profile seat and Liverpool would give him the chance to shine. Patrick however had the prudence to withdraw and T. P. O' Connor went on to win and hold the seat from 1885 until 1929. While T. P. O'Connor debated national and world events in the House of Commons and indulged himself in his journalistic prowess, Patrick Byrne in his own Council Chamber and on the streets, fought to improve the terrible social conditions of the poor of Liverpool. April 11, 1885 witnessed one of the most concentrated attacks on Patrick Byrne by 'The Liverpool Review' in a lengthy article when the wrote:

Dandy Pat's flare up, 'Och wirrasthru, tare an' blood an' thunder, bejabers, and the blessed mimory ov St. Patrick, ould Ireland and Donny Brooke fair, will some ov yez be good enough to tread on the tail ov me coat, for I'm blue mouldy for want ov a batin'.

Such might be imagined to have been the address of Dandy Pat to the astonished assembly of vestrymen as he pranced round the Law Association Rooms last Tuesday, flourishing a "bit of a stick," and trailing his black frock coat behind him. Whatever the vestrymen thought, they responded to his invitation by giving him a "batin" which ought to prevent him feeling "blue mould" for some time. The punishment administered of course, was of a moral and not of a physical nature and involved no corporal suffering on the part of the challenger, but it was nonetheless effective on that account. Being severely "sat upon" is almost as bad as being severely beaten and this was Dandy Pat's experience on the occasion in question.

However this may be, certain it is that Dandy Pat, made up his powerful mind to "flutter the Volscians" (People of ancient Italy, of unknown origin. The Volscians were subdued by the Romans in 338, BC) of the Vestry on Tuesday and in due course carried out his intentions. Whether the Volscians were as much fluttered as he expected them to be is a point on which our estimate and his would no doubt differ materially. Probably he thinks he cut rather a creditable figure on that occasion, thanks to the well-known, human incapacity to see ourselves as others see us. Less partial observers might be inclined to say that he answered to the traditional description of last month in that he "came in like a lion and went out like a lamb," and, it might be added, a lamb with its tail between its legs. Others might be disposed to suggest that his errand would have been more appropriately performed exactly a week ago, being singularly appropriate to the observances connected with the first of April.

The object of his embassy, in company with other compatriots, to the Vestry was to claim the election of another Roman Catholic member. Dandy Pat had made the wonderful discovery that the Irish constituted a third part of the population of Liverpool and claimed that they should have a representation on the Vestry in proportion to their numbers—that is eight out of twenty-four members. There are four Roman Catholics at present and though Dandy Pat contended that there ought properly to be eight, he was content to take another, making five in all, as a sort of instalment on account. As only himself and his companion, however, supported the proposal, it was easily defeated and another added to the "wrongs of Ireland". The wrong in this particular instance is not of a nature to excite very keen sympathy on the part of the unimaginative Saxon, or excite any feeling in him, beyond a flicker of passing amusement.

Dandy Pat is no doubt right in his assertion that the Irish constitute one-third of the total population of Liverpool, but as he asked himself what proportion they constitute of the ratepayers or householders? That there are a certain number of these at any rate in Vauxhall Ward is proved by the presence of Dandy Pat in the Council, but what about the vast majority of the twenty-three thousand or so Irish People, who have never been ratepayers or householders and in all human probability never will be, as long as they continue to spend their earnings in Scotland Road public houses, Dandy Pat's among the number. That people should claim to have a voice in the disposal of funds to which they never contribute, but from which they are always in a greater or less degree receiving assistance, is a specimen of Irish logic which is neither more or less then a bull of exceptional richness and absurdity.

The Dock Strike of 1887 was one of those occasions when Patrick Byrne immersed himself in trying to alleviate the suffering of dockers' families. A committee was set up for this purpose, headed by Hugh McAleavy, who lived among the poor of Liverpool. he at once enlisted the sympathy of Councillors Patrick Byrne, Purcell and George Jeremy Lynskey and these three formed themselves into a provisional committee. Letters were sent to a number of people whom they thought would respond to their invitation to assist in relieving the distress among the wives and children of the dock labourers on strike.

This relief movement was suggested and undertaken from humanitarian motives and entirely outside any idea of politics, religion or nationality. The result of this circular was a meeting at the Albert Hall, Liverpool, at which a sum of nearly £350 was subscribed, and a committee formed with the Rev. Father Dowling of St Anthony's as chairman and the first committee meeting was held at his presbytery. On the following day they decided to give immediate relief to the extent of £200 and the members of the committee were requested to seek out the most pressing cases. A member of the committee generously offered the use of a shop in Great Howard Street as headquarters for that day. A notice stating that relief would be given was put upon the shutters of the shop and when they arrived a large crowd of eager applicants, including men, women and children were already assembled in front of the premises. J. R. Grant, Liberal Councillor wrote:

> On the Saturday morning members of the committee with Mr. Pat Byrne, treasurer, who, I found, has a heart as big as his body and Mr. Purcell, the secretary, who was untiring in his devotion to the work, met at the office in Bevington Bush. It was pitiful to see the women and children who came to draw the five shillings in exchange for the tickets they had received. This was to me a sad experience. The women with pinched faces and the children pale and hungry would have touched any heart. It was wonderful how grateful they were. I think the Committee never received so many blessings as they did that day. I noticed that one member of the Committee quietly slipped an additional half-crown into the hand of one or two poor women and I have no doubt those other members did the same.

Up until Friday of last week it was unfortunately assumed that the relief movement was actuated by Party motives. I do not wonder that this impression should have got abroad, because the Committee up to this time composed of Pat Byrne and the majority of the subscriptions came from the persons of one political colour, the cause of this chiefly accidental. The three gentlemen who, in the first place, called together the meeting were Nationalists. No doubt this was in a large measure due to the district in which the principal served, however we soon satisfied two Conservative gentlemen that the charity was perfectly free from political or religious bias. Those two gentlemen were Mr. A. J. J. Bamford and Mr. Robert Foote and by their exertions we received a substantial addition to the funds. Mr. Pat Kearney has also done yeoman's service to the cause. Indeed, all the members of the Committee worked with marvellous industry from the beginning.

It must be fully understood that the Committee have not expressed any opinion upon the merits and demerits of the strike. Their work was purely philanthropic and they declined to embarrass themselves with any controversial questions. The relief Committee has meetings daily, some of these having lasted over three hours and some members have been so occupied with the work that they have been unable to attend to their own private business since the fund was started.

The subscription of one guinea sent by T. P. O'Connor, M.P., towards the relief of the Liverpool dockers' families, did not make a favourable impression. As most of the distress existed in and about the vicinity of the Vauxhall and Scotland Road area, which was T. P. O'Connor's constituency. By the beginning of 1888 at the age of forty-three Patrick Byrne was well on his way to becoming a wealthy man. He was by this time in control of twenty-three hotels and public houses in the

Merseyside area. Patrick may have had a more comfortable life style due to his hard work in business but he remained a thorn in the side of certain officials in the Council. Patrick continued to speak up on behalf of the poor and in the cause of Irish national politics. 'The Liverpool Review' Saturday, 4th February, 1888 stated:

Law and order are regarded as sacred by the Conservatives of the City Council--when it suits them. They don't mind a bit of a shindy when their opponents get the worst of it. The discussion which took place in the Council, on Wednesday, regarding the failure of the police to bring to justice the Orange Rowdies who attacked the Home Rule meeting in Scotland Ward and seriously injured Mr. Pat Byrne, shows this pretty plainly. Mr. Alder Livingstone, in particular, showed a bad spirit. He talked just as he was accustomed to talk a dozen years ago, when the Liberation Society's meeting in Hope Hall were subjected to attacks organised by the Orange Lodges.

The plain meaning underlying his speech is, that if a number of people hold a meeting at which speeches will be delivered distasteful to the Orangemen they must take the consequences. This is not the sort of tone to satisfy the public, or, we are glad to know, even, the bulk of the Conservative Party outside the Council. The Watch Committee must see that justice is done all round, if it is to receive the respect of decent citizens. It will not do for its members to be virtually indignant when National Leaguers are unruly and laugh in their sleeves when Protestant loafers commit an unproved and brutal assault on National Leaguers. What would the Conservatives have said of speeches like those of Mr. Livingston, Mr. John Hughes or Mr. Houlding if members of the majority party there had delivered them in the Dublin City Council, and the subject under debate had been an attack on a Unionist meeting by Catholic Home Rulers? In pandering to disorder because it is indulged in on their behalf. The

Conservatives of the City Council are playing with a two edged-sword.

Heated words continued to be exchanged in the Council Chamber, for example, in April 1888 a proposal to increase the salary of the Chief Constable, Captain Bower, from £850 to £1000 a year, was put before the council by the Watch Committee. Councillor Fred Smith objected to the increase as he found that a captain in the army received only 15s a day. Councillor Smith went on to speak of a market employee who had 45s a week and who had to rise in the morning at 4 o'clock but the committee would not raise his salary on account of economy. Dr. Bligh, Nationalist Councillor, said the captain would have been glad of half the salary a few years ago.

Councillor Patrick Byrne said that he could not forget that Mr. J. B. Smith held up his hands in holy horror, because a proposal was made to give a pension of 5s a week to an old and faithful servant who had been 46 years in the employ of the Corporation. He also quoted another case of a poor woman who had no one but a half-blind daughter to support her. He also alluded to the conduct of the police in making no arrests when he himself was so severely assaulted. Patrick Byrne furnished the names of nine of his assailants but the police made no arrests.

By 1889 'The Liverpool Review' had changed its stance on Patrick. It had accepted the view that he had a genuine concern for the town and its entire people when they interviewed him:

Mr. Pat Byrne and more widely and more genially known as "Dandy Pat", has been button-holed (interviewed) by a Review man about the Liverpool scavengers (refuse collectors) and wages. Mr. Byrne is not the fire-eater whom, judging by some of his speeches in the City Council, many people suppose. On the contrary, he is a quite, unassuming man, difficult to make talk of himself and wanting delicate handling by the interviewer. He is candid, however and speaks his opinions in a quite, earnest way, which carries conviction of his sincerity. The encounter between the Review and "Dandy Pat" took place last Tuesday in the famous "Morning Star Hotel", Scotland Place, Mr. Byrne's best-known house.

"You have been in the Liverpool City Council seven years have you not, Mr. Byrne and if I remember rightly you took up the question of the scavengers' wages almost as soon as you put your foot into the Council Chamber"?

"Yes, I consider the Liverpool scavengers the most ill-paid and depressed class of men in the corporate service. Their wages are a disgrace to a wealthy Corporation like Liverpool. I know a good many of the men, have visited them in their houses and all of that sort of thing and have been pained and shocked with their squalid surroundings—homes they cannot be called".

"And you have gone on pegging away at their grievances until, at the last council meeting, you practically won, or partly won, what you have been fighting for, for the last seven years"?

"Yes but on previous occasions the agitation in the Council has benefited the scavengers. You will remember that it was the custom to grant worn out scavengers a paltry few pounds when they got past work. Myself and other Councillors had those amounts of £5 and so on raised considerably in some cases to £20 or more, the grant now being increased with the length of time a scavenger has been in the corporate service. There is still one important move to be made in the matter of grants, though. At present the 'gift' is optional, we want to make it compulsory"?

"You had many more friends in the council at the last meeting to support your resolution then you ever had before"?

"I had, when I first took up the question I was almost single handed. I had great opposition to overcome and was, once threatened to be removed by the police from the Council Chamber when I was more than usually determined. Some members of the Council called loudly for my expulsion".

"Robert Durning Holt only took up the scavenger question as an advocate for the increased wages at the last Council meeting. He has been in the Council many years and seems to have only just now discovered the necessity of increased wages to the men. Holt stole your clothes, in fact. He knew you would move in the matter, I suppose"?

"Stole my clothes, eh? Well, I don't know about that. At all events increased wage for the scavenger is an accomplished fact and that is everything. No, I can't explain Mr. Holt's past inactivity in the matter, nor his sudden championship either. Nor can I account for the past tardiness of the Council to pay the men decently".

"How much do scavengers get a week"?

"Well they have to lose one day's work every alternative week. A full week's wage is 16s the one day less brings the money down to 13s 4d. Yes, the pay is 2s 8d a day or 14s 8d a week all round (Weekly pay for a sixty hour working week 14s 8d)".

"How many hours a day do the men work"?

"About twelve, they have to be at the Corporation store yards at five o'clock in the morning. They have a certain amount of work to do, so many streets to brush, you know and then they are finished".

"How much do you propose the increase shall be"?

"At least 2s. a week. The men were going to stand out for 4s a week, but the best course is perhaps to move little by little".

"But even with a rise of 4s a week their wages would still be under a £1".

"Quite so, but the ratepayers might object to a 4s rise. The total amount of the increase might look too large in the annual returns".

"Have the scavengers any other grievances beyond their starvation rate of pay"?

"A few, for instance, scavengers work in two sections. One lot 'finds the stuff' for the carts, the other lot fills it in. If a foreman at the yard thinks the load is a small one he can stop the scavengers engaged on that particular cartful a whole day's wages. The carter gets off with a fine of two pence".

"Are the men found in all requisites, brooms, shovels and the like".

"Yes, I think it only fair, however, that they should be provided with capes and leggings. If you saw them turning out on a cold winter's morning as I have, you would pity them from the bottom of your heart. They can't buy warm clothes out of their wages—how can men with families do so? And the consequences are they shiver through their work as best they can. The council votes thousands of pounds away in increased salaries to already over paid and not over-worked corporate officials and yet they are as close and niggardly as they can be to the poor starving scavengers."

"What class of men are put on as scavengers?"

"That is a point I would like to say something about. The men are of all ages, some young, and some old. Some have seen better days others have not. A large number are intelligent fellows, a few well read. A number, when they get past scavenging apply for jobs as night watchmen in the Corporation. But very often pensioners and absolute strangers are taken on as watchmen where old Liverpool scavengers are refused. Influence as a good deal to do with this and, to tell you the truth, it is openly said that the scavengers are worse treated because many of them are Irishmen. You would be surprised if you knew the difficulty there is with committees in getting Irishmen into the corporate employ, I have noted it very often."

"Do the men complain of their superiors?"

"From what I can gather Mr. Reynolds, the head of

the scavenging department, is very well liked by the men. They do, however, grumble about the way in which they are occasionally treated by the inspectors under Mr. Reynolds. I may say this, that some of the men have been in the service upwards of forty years. When a servant, in however subordinate and humble a capacity, has conducted himself well and done his work with satisfactorily for this length of time he is surely entitled to some consideration. The scavengers of Liverpool up to now have not had consideration. In the future we hope for a better state of things, at all events if things are not better for the men it won't be for the sake of trying. Success is practically assured now, though it as been a stiff fight for the past seven years."

"Just another word or two, Mr. Byrne we have mentioned St. Anne's Ward, what do you think of the present complication among, the Nationalists and Gladstonians (Liberals) there? You are perhaps the largest ratepayer in St. Anne's. How is the election going to turn"?

"We can win with a good man and we ought to win. I think the Irishmen in the ward are entitled to a fair hearing. But the suitability of any of the three men spoken of as a Liberal and Irish candidates, I have not quite made up my mind. We ought to get a man who knows the Ward thoroughly, a man who lives in the Ward. I think we can get such a man. But we must be united. It will never do to lose the chance of wrestling the seat from the Conservatives through selfishness or bickering on either side."

Patrick may not have had an abundance of friends in the Council Chamber however the local media could at times be much kinder. 'The Liverpool Citizen' showed this in an open letter to Patrick Byrne, 11th September 1889.

Patrick you're a broth of a boy—and I wish there were more like you! You are just one of the men I am more particularly proud of shaking hands with and doing my best to give fair play and justice to. You see, Patrick, you are open to many jibes and jeers, you are only a publican and you are chiefly associated with that gorgeous establishment in Scotland Place, very appropriately styled "The Morning Star." You are a self made man and a man of the people and therefore, a number of gentlemen who have never earned a penny in their lives, but live on the large fortunes and the small brains which their fathers have left them, may very easily find many ways of indulging in cheap sneers at your position.

Yet, Mr. Byrne, I feel proud to admit that there are few men who have risen from the ranks in the whole municipal history of Liverpool who have done their duty so contently, so bravely and yet with such unaffected modesty as yourself!

As you are aware, I have both scrutinised your votes in the Council and by your courtesy cross-examined you on them afterwards, but I am bound to confirm that though I have indulged in a little chaff— innocent chaff and criticism I trust you will admit— there are few men who have more steadily and honourably carried out their promises to the ratepayers who elected them.

As far as I can gather, you must have been in Liverpool about a quarter of a century. For twenty years past, I should think, you must have been trimming the light of that "Morning Star" of yours. And during all that time you appear to me to have conducted a most difficult business with success and, what is still more honourably, without reproach. Any fool who has a father can run a merchant's office, Pat. A great many very indifferent sorts of people can get on very well in a shop, but it takes a clever man to make his own first five-pound note as you did and carve out his own career, as you have done, in a walk of life, which is beset, with perils, temptations and dangers. And to come triumphantly at the end without a stain on his character, a useful public man and a thoroughly trustworthy representative of the working classes, from which I hope and believe, you are proud to have sprung.

Patrick, I have ventured to include you in my list of "Men in Danger" but, in the present instance, I am inclined to think that it is possibly your constituency, and not yourself that is in danger. It is said that you intend to retire? I am afraid you yourself are entitled to do so. You have a farm, Pat. Don't! Bother the pigs! There are plenty of Paddies to look after them. We want a few men of muscle and mind to look after the Aldermen! You've had what is really a jolly career for a son of old Erin – plenty of fighting and plenty of glory. And now you are safe in the haven of political rest, stick to your guns. Honestly, I don't know where we shall find another "Dandy Pat" if you go!

Look how straight your votes have been. You voted dead against that Vyrnwy Hotel. But, Pat, why in the name of fortune did you vote the other day for getting a licence for it? "Making the best of a bad job," say you? Yes, but if the thing's a bad job, why try to bolster it up? However, we can't agree upon every point, that's certain. On the other hand, Patrick, you were the first and best champion these poor Scavengers ever had. You voted for Sunday opening of the Gallery and Museum. You are against the Sunday Trading Prosecution Humbug. You were no pal of Leighton's Girl. You were in favour of every vote brought forward in the interests of the poorest of our fellow-citizens, and dead against almost every official "job" smuggled through or attempted. Patrick, I hate flattery; but you are really so well worth having in the Council that I should be sorry to see you snuff yourself out.

'The Liverpool Citizen' must have been aware of Patrick's plans to retire early due to his failing health possibly caused by the beatings inflicted upon him by political extremists. Patrick in private life was in many ways a lonely person. He was a single man who had put his business interests before the thoughts of wedded bliss. By 1889 his two brothers and sister had passed away, along with his parents. Moses, his father, was the last to die after having worked for many years helping his son in building up his business interests. Just a few months after the appearance of this article, Patrick Byrne was dead. Patrick died the 5th May 1890, aged 45. 'The Mercury' published an obituary the same day.

Mr. Patrick Byrne, one of the most respected of the Irish representatives in the Liverpool City Council, died this morning at his residence and place of business. 'The Morning Star', in Scotland Place. Mr. Byrne until quite recently was possessed of a vigorous constitution, which no amount of hard work seemed to shake.

He was the owner of several licensed houses in this district, and no more than a fortnight since he was proceeding from Rock Ferry to this city, when he had occasion to wait for a train. It was during the few minutes that he stood upon the railway platform that he caught a chill. This acted so seriously upon his general health that he determined to remain in bed the next day. The evil however, was never arrested, though every possible care was bestowed upon the patient, and though Dr. Wade had the further assistance and counsel of Dr. Carter.

Yesterday there was considered to have been an improvement in Mr. Byrne's condition, and in the evening he saw one or two friends, who remained in the sick chamber. However, no more than a few moments, towards one o'clock there was a change for the worse, whereupon Dr. Carter was summoned, but upon his arrival at 1-15 Mr. Byrne was breathing his last. The cause of death was pneumonia, which was the immediate and direct result of the cold. Mr. Byrne occupied a somewhat singular position in relation to the Irish party in Liverpool, and, though he was returned for Vauxhall Ward no more than six years ago, there was no one more closely acquainted with the needs and aspirations of his fellow countrymen.

It was the end of a dream and a sad day for the people of the Scotland Road and Vauxhall area. 'The Liverpool Daily Post' May 6, 1890, reported on some of the arrangements being made for the funeral:

The late Mr. Patrick Byrne—Yesterday the flag was flying at half-mast at the Town Hall, the Municipal Buildings, Dale Street and Free Library William Brown Street, in consequence of the death of Mr. Councillor Byrne. The flag was also at half-mast at the New Ferry pier. The funeral arrangements are as follows: the body will be removed from the "Morning Star Hotel", Scotland Place tonight to St. Joseph's Church, Grosvenor Street, where it will remain overnight. A requiem High Mass will be sung at ten o'clock to-morrow morning. The funeral cortege will leave the church at half-past three for the Prince's Land Stage and the remains will be put on board the Dublin boat, timed to sail at 6 p.m. The body will be interred at Mr. Byrne's native place—Ferns, County Wexford.

Mr. Byrne was forty-five years of age. At a specially convened meeting of the Michael Davitt Branch held at their rooms, 42 Richmond Row last night, Mr. D. Connolly in the chair, the following resolution was proposed by Mr. J. R. Grant and seconded by Mr. D. Mooney: "That we, the members of the Michael Davitt Branch, express our deep regret at the loss sustained by the Irish Party in Liverpool on the death of Mr. Councillor P. Byrne and we tender our sincere and heartfelt sympathy to his sorrowing friends." It was further proposed by, Mr. T. Mc Greavey and seconded by Mr. J. Hawkshaw, "That this branch present a floral wreath or cross to be placed on the coffin of the deceased." It was decided that a deputation from the branch should attend the funeral.

Groups of people congregated outside of the 'Morning Star' from early on and throughout the day, in total disbelief that their Dandy Pat had left them. During the day the crowd grew into thousands as they waited for the body to be removed and they followed in silence to St. Joseph's Church in the evening. It was a very impressive spectacle, showing the great loss that the surrounding community, in particular, had sustained by Patrick Byrne's death. Many stood in vigil at St. Joseph's all night. 'The Liverpool Mercury' 8th May reported on the funeral of the late "Mr. Byrne City Councillor".

Solemn Requiem Mass was celebrated yesterday morning at St. Joseph's Church, Grosvenor Street, for the repose of the soul of the late Mr. Patrick Byrne, City Councillor. The Church was draped in black and the benches and aisles were filled with people. The regret evidenced in this enormous concourse of mourners afforded conclusive evidence of the respect, esteem and affection, which Mr. Byrne won for him self during his career.

Many were the sighs and tears, which were to be heard above the beautifully impressive chanting by the choir priests who took part in the obsequies. The coffin containing the body of the deceased was covered with wreaths and flowers, which were after the service inspected by hundreds of tear dimmed eyes, mostly of the poor, so many of whom owe a deep debt of gratitude to Mr. Byrne. The Mass was sung by Fr. Roberts who was assisted by Frs. Blanchard and Griffin as Deacon and sub-Deacon, there were also present Fr. Dowling, Fr. Reynolds, Fr. Feeney, O.S.B., Fr. Ryan, O.M.I., Fr. Swarbrick, Fr. Park, Fr. Newsham, Fr. Brook, Fr. Ainscough and Fr. Frith.

Amongst the large congregation were Councillors Lynskey, Purcell, P.Kearney, D.Connelly, H. Mc Aleavey, F. Byrne, (Cousin of the deceased) C. H. Kelly, B. Hennin,

J. Prendiville, J. McArdle, J.Walker, P. Finnigan and Dr. Wade. There were also present Mrs. John Byrne (sister-in-law) Mrs. Hamner, Mrs. G Byrne, Mrs. Lambert, Mrs. Murphy and several other relatives and friends of the deceased. 'The Porcupine' wrote:

In the course of a few words addressed from the Altar, Fr. Roberts said that although Mr. Byrne was not a man who would like to have a funeral oration made over his body. He felt that the kindly heart, which now had ceased to beat, would not be averse to a few genuine words of respect. Fr. Roberts then spoke of the faithfulness with which Mr. Byrne had executed his official duties and the conscientious, energetic and fearlessly he had, of adhering to and expressing his opinions.

Even in the weakness of his illness, his thoughts were rambling over the duties of his position, which proved how his mind was laid upon them. The poor especially owed a tribute to the deceased and minute-by-minute they were learning how far his good deeds extended, deeds that none of them were aware of before. Living in the midst of the poor he could sympathise with them deeply and only a few weeks ago, the deceased was heard to say how his heart bled to see the suffering of some around him. Continuing, Fr. Roberts referred to the manful way in which the deceased had stood by his Church, his last good deed being an act of generosity in its favour. He was especially a lover of children and when told on his deathbed that the little ones were praying for him, his face lit up with joy and he said how great a blessing it was to have the prayers of the innocent children.

Fr. Roberts characterised the deceased as a genuine, frank-hearted, upright man who was during his lifetime determined to conscientiously do his duty. Fr. Roberts then gave a short sketch of Mr. Byrne's life and now he said, they were going to give him back to his native country, which he loved so well. That country might be proud of him, for none laboured more earnestly in her cause. Mr. Byrne was a most charitable minded man and scorned anything behindhand. Indeed the character of his opponents or of any one was safer behind their backs than in their presence with Mr. Byrne. In conclusion, Fr. Roberts urged them to testify their love for the departed by joining together in a Holy Sacrifice to God and pouring forth their prayers to God that He would give the deceased mercy. Remembering his charitable mind, the ardor of his faith and that He would shorten the time of his suffering, if he was in suffering and bring him into the bliss of Paradise.

About four o'clock in the afternoon the body was removed from St. Joseph's Church to the City of Dublin Steam Packet Company's steamer 'Kildare', which was moored at the Princes Stage and which left for Ireland at six in the evening. As already announced the internment will take place at Ferns, County Wexford today.

Long before the time appointed for the cortege to leave St. Joseph's, the line of the route was crowded with spectators and the children from the neighbouring Catholic schools, and a special body of police under Inspectors Tryers and McAuley arranged to keep the road clear. The route taken were the streets of the poor, Rose Place, Cazaneau Street, Juvenal Street, Scotland Road, Great Crosshall Street, Then on through the town along Hatton Garden, Dale Street, Water Street, to the Landing Stage. Business was almost entirely suspended between half past three and five o'clock in Scotland Road and the shutters of all the shops near to the 'Morning Star Hotel' were closed.

The blinds were also drawn down in the houses in Roe Place, Grosvenor Street and other thoroughfares through which the cortege passed. The coffin was covered with wreaths sent by friends and different branches of the Irish National League and it was conveyed to the Dublin steamer in an open hearse drawn by four horses. The Mayor's carriage followed. The procession comprised about fifty mourning and private carriages and in the front of the hearse walked the members of the associations with which the deceased was connected.

Among the clergy present were Frs. Roberts, Newsham, Blanchard, Griffin, Ainscough, Barry, Sheenan, Guinan and Cahill.

Cllrs. S. McMillin, J. G. Taggart, E. Purcell, G. J. Lynskey and H. C. Hawley were present, as also were Messrs. J. R. Grant, R. Thomas, D. Mooney, John Thomas, Thomas McGreevy, E. Phillips and J. D. Willis, representing the St. Anne's Ward Liberal Association.

The Local branches of the Irish National League were well represented. From the Joseph G. Biggar Branch there were Mr. P. Kearney, (president), Mr. E. Roche (vice president) and Messrs. J. B. Gribbin, Cusack, T. P. O' Reilly, Morris, Morrison, J. D.Willis, Buckley, Barber, Phillips, Lyons, R. Roche, J. C. Clarke, T. Hart, L. Hart, O'Connor and the honorary secretary, (Mr. John Gould). Messrs, Loughran, B. Fay, M. Farrell and P. Corrigan. St. Pauls' Branch: Messrs, E.Wall, (president) T. Maher, P. Fitzsimmons, E. Cannon and J. Fitzpatrick.

West Toxteth branch: Messrs. J Daisey, (President), H. O'Neill, J. O'Rourke and T. Kelly. The Parnell Branch, Messrs, A Maybury (president) E.Tiernan, E. McCann and B. O.Kane. Old Swan Branch: Messrs, J. Galvin (president), C. McGuire, J. Dolan and D. Morrissey. North branch, Messrs, E. Purcell, (president), O'Mahony, Burke and James.

Central branch: Messrs, T. Kelly, T. Kilcoyne, B. M'Coy, Quirke, Dunne, P. Kelly and O. O'Hara. North branch: D. Connelly, (president), J. Barry, (vice president), D. Leary, (hon. treasurer), T. Joyce, (Hon secretary). J. R. Grant, H. McAleavy, J. Hawkshaw, M. Reynolds, W. Carroll, J. J. Morgan, J. Mulgrew, P. Ratichan, C. Kenny, W. Henry, T. M'Greavy, R. Thomas, J. Thomas, D. Mooney, L. Kenny, M. Kenny, M. Reynolds and J. Broderick. Michael Davitt, Branch and The Irish National Foresters were

111

represented by Messrs, Willis, Sexton, Monaghan, Cassidy, Reynolds, McGreavy and Murphy.

The Liverpool Licensed Victuallers Association were represented by Messr. T. Braniley, (Chairman), F. Armstrong, C. J. O'Connor, T. Robinson, J. Pye, Harrison and J. Leach (secretary). Also at the Church, were W. Carroll, J. Willis, T. Maher, E. Brooks, A. Gould and Mr. Jones, (secretary of the Exchange Liberal Association) Charles H. Kelly, J. A. King and J. Thomson, (secretary) of the Constitutional Association). C. McCann, J. Wade, G. L. Baker, J. Hamill, H. Neale, J. Neill, J. McDonald, D. Mooney, B. Hemmin, F. H. Gilbert, T. W. Outhwaite and W. Allison, (Ind, Coope and Co). J. Thomas, (West Toxteth Liberal Association) H. F. Read, J. Ellison, M. McEvoy, H. P. Boulnois (city engineers).

Mr. J. M. King master of the Prince's Landing Stage had some 400 feet of the stage roped off, leaving just one bridge entirely free to the mourners who arrived at this point at about five o'clock. Here again was an immense crowd of people anxious to catch a glimpse of the coffin and Inspectors Lanigan and Simpson, in charge of a large body of constables, had no easy task in keeping the spectators from rushing towards the "Kildare" whose commander was Captain Conlon. The flag was flying at half-mast at the stage master's cabin. Fr. Roberts, who was to conduct the burial service at Ferns, accompanied the chief mourners to Ireland. Mr. Thomas Maguire, of Mount Street carried out the funeral arrangements in Liverpool.

At the meeting of the city council the Mayor (Mr. T. Hughes) on taking the Chair, said:

> Before proceeding to the business of the day it is my painful duty to call attention to the fact that one of our members has been called away by death. You will all know that Mr. Patrick Byrne who has been a member of this Council for some years has, in the prime of his life, been called away to his last rest. I am quite sure it will be your wish to express your deep sympathy for

the loss, which his family and friends have sustained, and to mark our sense of loss to this Council.

Mr. Byrne was a gentleman well known to you all and although not, perhaps, largely interested in the work of our committees, still he did take a kindly interest in one or two of those committees and especially in the work of the Insanitary Property Committee of which he had a practical knowledge. But I think he will be best remembered by the kindly interest he always took in the poorer employees of this Corporation. For we know and we shall never forget, the kindly sympathy, which he always expressed towards those poorer men and how he strove to ameliorate their conditions and certainly did his best to promote their interest. It is with feelings of this kind that we think of him to-day and we cannot help feeling deep sympathy with those friends whose mournful duty it will be to follow his remains to the banks of our river, whence the pass over for internment to his native isle. I am sure you will feel it our duty to mark the sense of the loss sustained and our condolence with his friends and I will call upon the Chairman of the Finance Committee to move a formal resolution.

Alderman W. Radcliffe said it was only at the last meeting of the council that the late Mr. Byrne was present and took part in the deliberations. During the seven years he was connected with the Council he was very consistent in his conduct, particularly in furthering the interest of his poorer brethren and in an unassuming manner. Mr. Radcliffe moved, "that this Council receive with regret the announcement of the death of Patrick Byrne, Esq., who for some years took an active part in the business of this Council. and that the Mayor be requested to convey to the relatives of the late Mr. Byrne this sincere expression of the sympathy and condolence of the council with them in their bereavement." Mr. J. B. Smith seconded the motion, which was unanimously carried.

T. P. O'Connor sent a telegram "Please convey my deep sympathy and my great sorrow at the death of a staunch and brave Irishman."

After the death of Patrick Byrne the outline of his will was made known. Bequests were made to St. Joseph's Church, Holy Cross Church, St. Anthony's Church, St. Francis Xavier's and other Churches in the area. Every one of his employees received £5 each with an addition of £5 for every year that they had spent in his service. As one man had twenty-two years in his service, his bequest amounted to £115. He also left a bequest to the Liverpool Seamen's Orphanage. Patrick also helped the poor of Ferns, his birthplace and then left the residue of his estate to his two nieces, his nephew, and his sister in-law in Ferns.

A movement was set up to commemorate his charity and his sympathy with the poor of Liverpool. 'The Liverpool Review' Saturday, May 25th published an article:

> The Byrne Memorial mentioned remarkable gratitude of Liverpool labourers. The Patrick Byrne Memorial Fund promises to be one of the most truly popular of anything of the kind ever promoted in this city. At the inaugural meeting a sum of £50 was subscribed in the room among a score of people. At the first committee meeting, held on Tuesday evening last, the secretary of the Scavengers' Union stated that the scavengers of Liverpool, as a mark of gratitude to the late Mr. Byrne, were desirous to subscribe each of them, three pence a week for four weeks towards the Fund. The hon. treasurer of the Dock Labourers' Union also informed the meeting that the various branches of the Union are to be called together to consider the best mode of supporting the memorial.
>
> Although no one had been out collecting funds, the chairman and treasurer of the fund received promises of an additional £18 at the committee meeting. It has not yet decided what form the memorial is to take, whether it is to be a public fountain, a bed in a

hospital, or a statue. but there is a general feeling that the memorial should be localised among the people where Mr. Byrne's life and labours were spent. It is to be hoped that whatever form the memorial may take, it will be a practical and useful form, and thus be in keeping with the general work and object of Mr. Byrne's life. After much discussion and deliberation by the memorial committee, it was proposed that the memorial should take the form of a water fountain. It also proposed that it be erected in Scotland Place, opposite Mr. Byrne's "Morning Star Hotel".

Monument erected to Councillor Patrick Byrne.

The fountain of red Aberdeen granite in memory of Councillor Patrick Byrne was erected in 1892, and sited outside of the 'Morning Star Hotel'. Later it was moved from Scotland Place because of road widening and placed in Pownall Square, where vandalism took its toll. In 1983 it was put into a Corporation yard, but sadly disappeared. An article in 'Ireland's Own' January 1998, telling the story of Dandy Pat created renewed interest in the life of Patrick Byrne. "The Dandy Pat Memorial

Project" was formed to try and find the remains of the fountain, and after an appeal by the 'Scottie Press Community Newspaper' the base of the fountain was found with an inscription still visible:

Erected in Memory of Patrick Byrne City Councillor who was distinguished for his services to the Ratepayers, benefactions to the Poor, and ardent love of his Native Land died 5th May 1890 Interred at Ferns, Co Wexford.

Design and Draughtmanship by Michael Kelly.

The new Byrne monument incorporating the original base was unveiled in the grounds of St Anthony's Church Scotland Road, thanks to Canon Tom Williams who kindly gave permission to have it placed there. The Lord Mayor of Liverpool, Councillor Joe Devaney, unveiled the monument on Friday 14 April 2000. Also in attendance were Louis Ellman M.P. and a representative of the Irish Embassy along with Fr. Tom Williams, St. Anthony's Church, Rev. Steve Williams, Liverpool Parish Church of Our Lady and St. Nicholas, Councillor Pauline Connolly and Councillor Marie McGiveron of the Vauxhall Neighborhood Council. Members of Dandy Pat Project, Bernard Morgan, Joe O'Grady, Tom Walsh, Ron Formby and Michael Kelly. The 'Echo Wexford' also keeps alive the memory of this champion of the poor:

The Lord Mayor of Liverpool, Councillor Joe Devaney
unveiling the monument

Pat Byrne rests in Ferns Old Cemetery. The Irish people and those of Irish descent in Liverpool in the latter half of the 19th century were favoured by having one of the noblest leaders and kindest friends that enforced emigrants could desire. Born in Ferns parish two years prior to that awful era of plague in Ireland, 'Black '47', Pat emmigrated to Liverpool as a youth. His first occupation in that leading great seaport was that of a Docker.

Pat Byrne's final resting place in Ferns Old Cemetery, Ireland.

11
John Byrne J.P.

In the eighteenth, and nineteenth, century, Wexford sent to Liverpool many outstanding people, and not least of these were John Byrne and his family. He was born in Wexford in 1846. and entered Liverpool while still in his teens. At the age of seventeen he enrolled himself in the Brigade of Artillery Volunteers, which at that time provided their own uniform. It is more than possible that he was acquainted with Patrick Byrne, (Chapter 10) if not a relation of his they would have arrived in Liverpool, from Wexford around the same time. They were both teenagers with only a year difference, in their age. Both men later served Liverpool on the Town Council.

After leaving the Army John Byrne founded a high-class and well known firm of jewellers and silversmiths located in Bold Street. His high-class jewellers which was extensively patronised by the well-to-do of Liverpool. 'The Post and Mercury' wrote. "In Liverpool, no tradesman was better known among the people of St Peter's Ward, his name was a household word. He was one of the oldest and largest ratepayers in the city".

He successfully contested the seat for St. Anne's Ward in 1896, to serve on the 'Select Vestry'. He became Chairman of the Schools Committee and Chairman of a special committee appointed by the 'Select Vestry', to consult with the Watch Committee on methods to relieve the streets of neglected children. In 1897 John Byrne became its chairman in 1909 was elected to the City Council for St. Peter's ward. He became a member of the Library Museum and Arts Committee. He retired from the council in 1912. Although he served the town well he never lost his love of Ireland and kept himself informed on the political situation in the country.

His eldest son Myles Emmet Byrne was Colonel of the 5th 8th Irish Regiment and was later in command of one of the Irish Battalions of the Northumberland Fusiliers. 'The Liverpool Review', September 1903 in a profile of Myles Emmet Byrne:

There is perhaps no Volunteer officer in the service of King Edward V11 who has risen by sheer merit from Subaltern to Lieutenant-Colonel with greater rapidity than Colonel Myles Emmet Byrne, the commanding officer of the 5th V.B. (Volunteer Brigade) (Irish). He served for a period in Ireland and commanded a company of the Royal Irish Militia, after which he gained great experience as acting adjutant of the L.I.V. (Liverpool Irish Volunteers) and the duties of that position were ably discharged by him for a considerable period. He succeeded Colonel Caruthers in the command, and during the Boar War the 'Fighting Fifth' (Fighting Fifth Irish) sent out no fewer than 250 officers, non-commissioned officers and men for active service in South Africa.

John Byrne's second son, Dr. Thomas Wafer Byrne, was a City Councillor for Sandhills Ward. A third son was a dental Surgeon in London.

John Byrne died on 26, November 1915. A host of friends of all shades of politics and religion heard with regret of his death at his home Clermist, in Greenbank Road, Sefton Park, Liverpool. A Requiem Mass was celebrated for his repose of the deceased at St Clare's Church, Arundel Avenue, Sefton Park, Liverpool. Interment took place in Allerton Cemetery.

12

T. P. O'Connor
Journalist Politician

----The poor, the weak, the beaten require the work of every human man and woman to stand between them and the world.

Thomas Power O'Connor, more commonly known as 'Tay Pay' by his friends, was the son of Mr. Thomas O'Connor, of Athlone. His mother was Theresa, daughter of Mr. Thomas Power, formerly of the Connaught Rangers. Tay Pay was born in 1847 and educated at the college of the Immaculate Conception, Athlone and Queen's College, Galway and Graduated M.A. at Queen's University Belfast.

Thomas had three sisters, Teresa born 1850, Eleanor Julia, born 1852 and Mary born in 1859. He also had a brother Jack, baptised John Joseph in 1854. His parents had a substantial terraced house in the centre of Athlone, in Castle Street. Thomas first entered the world of journalism with the Dublin based 'Saunders' Newsletter', about 1867 and was given a salary of £2 a week. In 1870 the budding writer left Ireland to try and develop the skills of journalism in Fleet Street, London.

Thomas landed his first job with the 'Daily Telegraph' but it was only a brief stay. Tay Pay, as he had become known, felt he was entitled to more money and like Oliver Twist with his begging bowl, asked for more and was shown the door. Tay Pay was a very resilient character and within a few days became the London correspondent for the 'New York Herald' at £5 a week but his services were dispensed with after just eighteen months due mainly to a downturn in the fortunes of the 'New York Herald'. For the next six or seven years, until 1879, Tay Pay experienced the fear brought about through unemployment and was glad to pick up the crumbs of the occasional assignment. Life might have been a little insecure in the 1870s but it did not stop Tay Pay from acquiring an M. A. from Galway in 1873. He recalled the hunger of an unemployed journalist when he wrote:

> I had all the experiences that ever befell the old authors in Grub Street, (London). I had often to go without food, and still remember the envious eye, with which I passed the shops with sausages and mashed potatoes. I got some odd jobs now and then, some of them how ridiculous! Once I wrote weekly imaginative accounts of the great prizefights of old. I had to draw the line at a description of the rounds, those were done for me by a fellow-Irishman—a doctor—who was an excellent amateur boxer. The paper got a good circulation—mainly through these picturesque prizefights. I never saw, and never would see, a prizefight. Next I tried my hand at a penny dreadful, and a correspondent of mine who remembers the wretched thing assures me that the climax of each instalment was seductive and thrilling. What I most remember is the thirty-five pounds I got for it was very welcome.

The thirty-five pounds did not elevate Tay Pay to new heights, as the days of hunger days still haunted him and he recalled the loneliness of his empty pockets.

In the midst of these horrors, and in a single-room I occupied in an Islington lodging-house, I found myself on a Saturday evening with just three half pence in my pocket. And in my hands a letter which began with a cold "Dear Sir", and was the breaking-off of an engagement to a woman whom I had regarded as the centre and only hope of the world to me.

Although his heart was broken, his spirit was not and he soon found an appointment as sub-editor to the 'London Echo'. However the long hours of six at night until three in the morning did not suit him and he moved on to find greener pastures. Tay Pay would look back on the hard times in London with a nostalgic and philosophical eye. "Looking back on that terrible time, I can re-create the tragic phases in the lives of so many literary men. Their habits exacted their toll, and I do not think I exaggerate when I say that fifty years was about the average expectation of life with the journalists of my early days".

Many of the public houses in London were a great attraction to Tay Pay and his journalist colleague's nightly debates on all manner of subjects would take place. For the aspiring politician like Tay Pay it was a chance to put his point of view forward and practice the art of public speaking. Coger's Hall was one such place that had nightly debates, but the 'Green Dragon' was Tay Pay's favourite. "It would require the pen of Balzac to draw portraits of the strange, hopeless, fallen creatures I used to meet almost nightly at these oratorical jousts". There were several good speakers among them and he recalled them when he wrote:

One of them was a barrister, a fine looking man with a splendid presence and very fine oratorical powers. He was reputed to be a near relation of a great figure who was then in the Ministry or was about to be a Cabinet Minister. Our barrister was a typical Englishman. There was an equally typical Scotsman, who had written several books and spoke with all the logic characteristic of his race, but his features showed the unmistakable sign of dissolute habits.

There was an Irishman, of course, his name was Finlan and for an hour he had played a notable part. He was a small, rather good-looking man. Anyhow he was a brilliant debater—indeed, the chief pillar of the debates—and he was a brilliant fellow. I remember the effect it had on me when, seeing him looking unusually well and unusually steady, I asked him for the explanation. He then told me that he had got a job at his trade, which was that of a French-polisher, he seemed quite happy, Ultimately he disappeared to America and never to be seen again.

The importance of these nights to me was that I got a hard training in speaking. The subject on which I spoke most often was Home Rule, then beginning to be taken seriously. On that subject I had to stand up to all kinds of people. One of my opponents was an old college chum who came from the North of Ireland, and, though a Liberal, was a violent opponent of Home Rule. My countrymen in London began to hear me, and I got innumerable invitations to address meetings—especially in public houses, where I was regarded by the proprietors as a useful addition to their power of attracting customers.

Tay Pay resolved to try for the position of publisher's reader but was persuaded by the publisher, S. O. Beeton to write a book on the life of Disraeli. However he was a little unsure of his own literary ability.

I have often thought that it was something of a handicap to begin in the lower ranks of the profession. At least, it was so in those days, and a reporter who would try for anything editorial was somewhat like the ballet girl who would demand the place of a prima donna. I shared the prejudice against myself; and when anyone proposed to me to write a book I felt as unnerved as though I had been offered the command of the Channel Fleet.

Tay Pay spent three years working on his book, while still without permanent employment but at last his book was published 1879. 'The Spectator' gave him a long and laudatory review and 'The Standard' gave him a long but fiercely hostile review. The book's critical portrait of Disraeli came at the right time for Tay Pay with a new election looming. 1880 was to bring a big change in the fortunes of Tay Pay when he was elected to Parliament for Galway and he later looked back on this period with great satisfaction:

> I dwell on these adventures, first to give some idea of the kind of man the voters in Galway approached when, just as I had turned thirty-two years of age, I sat in my squalid chambers in Barnard's Inn, secondly, to enforce the proposition that, in spite of my youth, I had already some of the professional training of a man who was destined for political life. Again and again, in the course of my writings, I have insisted, as the result of my experience, that the gift of speaking requires constant, almost uninterrupted, practice. The more frequently a speaker speaks, the better as a rule, he speaks. That applies even to the greatest masters of oratory. I watched Gladstone in the House of Commons practically every night for nearly twenty-years and I had to watch him as a journalist, ever ready to pounce for material to enliven my nightly sketches on Parliament. I can say confidently that there was scarcely a sketch I wrote during this long period in which he did not supply me with much, sometimes all, of my copy.

During Tay Pay's early days as a young reporter in Dublin earning £2 pound a week, he decided to bring his two sisters and younger brother to live with him. "I have written more than once, that every Irishman is born with a family, especially if he be the eldest son and gives a promise of a more prosperous future than that of his hard drive-parents". Tay Pay would often look back on those days, as a struggling reporter as the happiest days of his life.

Tay Pay being the bright and ambitious man that he was, his eyes were cast towards a more profile seat where his parliamentary and journalist talents could shine. Liverpool Scotland Division needed an Irish Nationalist for the parliamentary seat in the general election 1885. It was up for grabs and Tay Pay was determined to be first past the post. Only one man stood in his way – this was Patrick Byrne, chosen by the majority of the Nationalist organisations in Liverpool. The later was the benefactor, the hope of a better future for the thousands of poor in the Scotland Division, and he was familiar their poverty and aspirations. He had served them well as their representative on the Liverpool Council. Now Pat Byrne had to stand to one side to let this thirty-eight year old up-start and favourite of Parnell go forward. Yet Tay Pay in Parliament and London was well cushioned against the crying needs of his constituents back in Liverpool.

He was thought to be a lazy parliamentarian, a more or less indifferent or lethargic patriot, but a tremendous journalist working at tiptop pressure and more of a journalist than a politician. At one time he was responsible for the London letter of the 'Liverpool Daily Post'. This gave him a platform on home rule for his Liverpool audience, which he would reel off with a vengeance. He was one of the most effective and scathing of the band of Home Rulers in the House of Commons when they were fighting against Liberals and Tories alike. During those exchanges he still found time to pen leaders and specials for metropolitan and provincial newspapers amid all the whirl of political life.

He penned a magnificent series of articles on Ireland and the Irish question, contributed to the 'Ha'Penny Week', a journal run in conjunction with the 'Liverpool Mercury'. According to 'The Liverpool' Post:

It is difficult to say anything new to Liverpool folks about T. P. O'Connor. He has been before the public for so long a time in a three-fold capacity, so much has been written about him in this and that journal, and he, as been interviewed so frequently, that probably "Tay Pay" himself, with all his ingenuity, ability and resource, couldn't say a brand new thing about himself. And busy, bustling, and brilliant as he is, he possibly wouldn't if he could. Privately, the member for the Scotland Division of Liverpool at St. Stephen's is steeped to the lips in originality, and he has a rich and perhaps inexhaustible fund of personal reminiscences calculated to delight the heart of a bohemian of the bohemians. It should be remembered, too, that Mr. O'Connor is practically a teetotaler and a non smoker, he lives in, for, and with his work.

There is a story of O'Connor to the effect that when he was writing the book which most people consider his finest effort, 'Beaconsfield and his Times', he was living hard up in a Fleet Street garret, so hard up that he had to borrow the wherewithal to procure a clean collar and a two-eyed-steak. The former he wanted to wear at the publisher's when he was handing in his "copy," and nature demanded something, anyhow, to sustain the young Napoleon of journalism physically, while his reputation was growing. This may be a mere yarn, but it is good, or bad, enough to be true. More than once the writer has heard the subject of this sketch dilate upon his earlier up-hill experiences. "They call me 'Tay Pay'," he says, "I wish that some of them that do and who are so darned familiar with my patronymic had had some of my climbing to do." This is again characteristic.

Scotland Division's member doesn't look for fawning, or yarning, or familiarity. He's too serious an Irishman in every feeling and timbre and fibre, and trained in the Queen's College Galway, he launched out on the sea of London journalism when he was a lathe of a lad. He subsequently had hard times of it financially and in other ways, but his indomitable pluck and perseverance, no less than his ability, kept him going and progressing. Then he jumped into or was sucked into the whirlpool of politics. What a name he has made therein everybody knows. He is not great or loyal or even considerate as a parliamentary representative. His constituency and his constituents very seldom see him, and he is frequently absent from the House, but he is a superb political debater.

In inches of stature and girth, T.P. O'Connor is more than the average man, as in intellect and capacity he leaves many of his confreres far behind him. All the while O'Connor was engaged in other newspaper ventures and, was one of the most alert, forcible, and eloquent champions of Home Rule in the House of Commons and out of it. The British Isles and America can testify to this fact.

His association with the 'Star', 'Sun', and the 'M.A.P.' are too recent to require comment. At the moment he is an undeniable force journalistically and politically, and those who go to hear him speak in the Rotunda Theatre on Sunday next will have rich treat his burning eloquence and his rhetoric always strike home. Gifted with humour, oratorical ability, and having a cynical, not to say sardonic vein, he is bound to be attractive. He may not have achieved greatness either as writer or as speaker, but he has forced his way to the front as a celebrity by sheer weight of worth, if one may so put it.

In Liverpool T.P. is an unfamiliar figure. But when he does take into his head to visit the banks of the Mersey and address a meeting he is usually at his very best. That is to say, he has a text upon which he speaks very fluently, and, yes boldly. With folded arms, a musically modulated voice, and heroic bearing, he will talk for a couple of hours splendidly, learnedly, and convincingly. You wish you had opportunities of hearing the man more frequently. He draws you irresistibly to him while he is speaking, and you cheer him to the echo when he has sat down after his peroration. Yet there is something wanting. You feel, somehow, that O'Connor is "a man on his own," a man not born of politics, a man who doesn't take political life as seriously as he takes it in other ways.

When you judge him from that angle you may be doing him an injustice, for he is one of the most useful, correct, wholesouled men of the day. If he does no more for Ireland, politics, a higher grade of public life, journalism, and humanitarianism, he has done his share. Among Liverpool's nine M.P.s he is the most widely known and the most universally popular. In the House of Commons he is a force—not a fighting force now—but a force that tends for progress and for good.

Thomas Power O'Connor founded the 'The Star' in 1887, and Henry Hamilton Fyfe, was a reporter on the 'Times' when he read the first edition of 'The Star':

> I recollect very well reading the first number of T. P. O'Connor's, The Star (that was in 1888) I read it over my cocoa and aerated bread lunch-with excited enjoyment. T. P. O'Connor, a journalist of genius reality was the founder of new journalism, which ousted those dull morning papers. Ten years afterwards, his Star offered good reading from many pens, some already famous, some to be. He was bold enough to declare a policy of justice for the underdogs. "The rich, the privileged, the prosperous", he wrote, "need no guardian or advocate. The poor, the weak, the beaten require the work of every human man and woman to stand between them and the world."

Henry Hamilton Fyfe was later appointed editor of the 'Daily Mirror', and in 1922 he became editor of the 'Daily Herald'. Tay Pay offered the position of an assistant editor of 'The Star' to Mr. H.W. Massingham who was then working for a small syndicate agency. Tay Pay commenting on Massingham's great ability in the world of journalism said. "For the first time his brilliant pen got a real scoop. He used to talk with rapture of a gentleman whose name neither I nor anybody else had ever heard before, his name was George Bernard Shaw. He was one of the assistant leader-writers". Earnest Parke was another appointee of 'The Star'. Of him, Tay Pay wrote:

> I was recommended by Sir John Robinson, of the "Daily News" to a young man named Earnest Parke, then working in the office of a city newspaper. Ernest Parke was then a young, floss man, with a keen face, a lithe and agile body, a tremendous flair for news, and capable of hours of work, if necessary, in a single day. He was, as he is, a singular mixture of shrewdness and ideals and intense radical, and at the time a thoroughly practical journalist.

Ernest Parke increased the circulation of 'The Star' due to the reporting of the 'Jack the Ripper' case. 'The Star' also had the distinction of introducing a regular political cartoon. The paper ran for seventy-three years ceasing publication in 1960.

In 1888 Elizabeth Howard, an American went to Ireland, where she met and married Tay Pay. They lived in London, where they published 'The Star' newspaper, and socialised in political and literary circles. Among their acquaintances and friends were George Bernard Shaw, Oscar Wilde, Brete Harte, Arthur Conan Doyle, Henry James and Ellen Terry. Searching for an independent source of income, she wrote and starred in a play, 'The Lady from Texas' (1901), but it failed. She also wrote another 'The Last Leader', but there is no indication that it was ever produced. Her books included the Autobiographical 'I Myself' in 1910, 'Little Thank You' in 1912, 'My Beloved South' in 1913, 'Dog Stars' in 1915, 'Herself Ireland' in 1917 and 'The Hat of Destiny' in 1923.

In 1916 Tay Pay was appointed to the post of Film

Censor. When he was appointed President of the British Board of Film Classification, one of his first tasks was to give evidence to the Cinema Commission of Inquiry, set up by the national Council of Public Morals in 1916. He summarised the Board policy by listing forty-three grounds for deletion laid down for the guide of examiners. This list was drawn from the Board's annual reports 1913-1915. and shows the strictness felt necessary if the Board was to earn the trust of the public and relevant bodies. It is worth looking at just some of them on the list for deletion.

Unnecessary exhibition of under-clothing.
Nude figures.
Offensive vulgarity and impropriety in conduct and dress.
Indecorous dancing.
Excessively passionate love scenes.
Bathing scenes passing the limits of propriety.
References to controversial politics.
Relations of capital labour.
Realistic horrors of warfare.
Subjects dealing with India, in which British Officers are seen in an odious light, and otherwise attempting to suggest the disloyalty of Native States or bring into disrepute British prestige in the Empire.

Thomas Power O'Connor died in 1929, his wife Elizabeth O'Connor died two years later in London on September 1, 1931 and was buried in Surrey. There are people around who still remember Tay Pay riding in his open landau pulled by two teams of horses. He would ride around his kingdom of the Scotland Division waving his silk hat from his carriage, looking for all the world like the Lord Mayor.

13

Percy French
Songwriter, Entertainer, Poet and Painter

Percy French may not have lived in Liverpool or its environs but he does have connections with the area. William Percy French was born on 1, May 1854 at Cloonyquin House, County Roscommon, Ireland. His childhood was spent in a comfortable middle-class background. Percy's father, Christopher French was a landlord and his mother, Susan Emma, came from Carrick-On-Shannon. She was the daughter of the Rev. William Percy, Rector of the town. The French family was descended from one of the merchant tribes of Galway but the changing social and economic climate after 1850, brought about a decline in their fortunes.

Known to his family and friends as Willie, Percy entered Trinity College, Dublin, in 1872 to study civil engineering. Instead of focusing on academic matters, he began to develop his remarkable talents for songwriting, dramatics, banjo playing and watercolour painting. In 1877 he wrote a song, 'Abdulla Bulbul Amear', for a college concert, which was so successful that he published it. Not having registered the copyright of the song it was pirated and became an even greater hit, but without financial benefit to the author.

After an unusually long number of years French emerged from university with an engineering qualification. He was about to emigrate to Canada in 1883 when he obtained a post on a government drainage scheme in County Cavan. While in the post of 'Inspector of Drains', he found time to develop his interest in music and drama together with watercolour painting. His time spent in Cavan, which came to an abrupt end in 1888, provided inspiration for two of his great songs, 'Phil the Fluter's Ball' and 'Slattery's Mounted Foot'. Percy took himself off to Dublin and was for two years editor of a comic weekly magazine 'The Jarvey'. He used this medium to promote a series of concerts throughout Ireland under the banner of 'The Jarvey Concert Company' and to advertise his ever-increasing output of comic songs. Following the demise of the 'The Jarvey', Percy, never far from the footlights, provided the libretto and played the leading role in two comic operas (music by his friend and collaborator Dr. W. H. Collisson). In 1891 Percy French was to suffer the loss of his young wife, Ettie, who died in childbirth just one year and one day after their marriage. Their baby daughter also died some days later. In 1892 Percy married his second wife Helen (Lennie) Sheldon of Burmington House Warwickshire, England. They had three daughters, Ettie, Mellie and Joan who was the last surviving daughter and died in 1996.

In 1896 Percy turned to the stage for a full time career and encouraged by a friend and partner, Richard C. Orpen, he became known as W. Percy French. He wrote, produced and played the major parts in a topical revue called 'Dublin Up To Date', consisting of sketches, caricatures, stories and songs. This show was to form the basis of a stage entertainment that would be his future fame and livelihood. In 1900, following ever greater acclaim in Ireland and now known professionally as 'Percy French' he went to the richer pastures of London.

136

Having played successfully in the theatres and music halls of the populous cities of Britain the career of Percy French as an entertainer reached its zenith. He and Dr. Collision toured Canada, U.S.A. and the West Indies in 1910 and received enthusiastic notices in the major cities of the west coast. Percy also toured the ski resorts of Switzerland from time to time and although based in London from 1900, he returned to play the holiday resorts and towns of Ireland every year. For relaxation Percy continued to develop his love of watercolour painting. He painted prolifically and often paid for his board and lodgings with his paintings.

Not known for a desire to accumulate money, he sometimes just gave his paintings to friends or acquaintances. His most sought after scenes depicted the light and character of the Irish landscape in its most evocative moods. This activity left a colourful record of his tours as an entertainer in Switzerland, Canada, U.S.A. and the West Indies.

A collection of Percy's watercolours is in the care of The Percy French Society at the North Down Heritage Centre in County Down, Ireland. His feelings for the west of Ireland, is evident in his poem 'To The West':

The Midland Great Western is doing its best,
And the circular ticket is safe in my vest,
But I know that my holiday never begins
Till I'm in Connemara among the Twelve Pins.
The Bank has no fortune of mine to invest
But there's money enough for the ones I love best,
All the gold that I want I shall find on the whins
When I'm in Connemara among the Twelve Pins.
Down by the Lough I shall wander once more'
Where the wavelets lap lap round the stones on the
shore:
And the mountainy goats will be wagging their chins
As they pull at the bracken among the Twelve Pins.
And its welcome I'll be, for no longer I'll meet
The hard pallid faces I find in the street,

The girl with blue eyes, and the boy with brown shins,
Will stand for their pictures among the twelve Pins.
To night, when all London's with gaslight agleam,
And the Carlton is filled with society's cream',
I'll be 'takin' me tay' down at ould Johnny Flynn's
Safe and away in the heart o' the Pins.

On completion of an engagement in Glasgow in 1920
Percy French fell ill so he took the train to Liverpool to
board the Packet Steamer for Dublin. Percy was not able
to join the steamer, as he was too weak, so he made his
way to the home of his cousin the Rev. Richardson at
Formby were he died a few weeks later. The people of
this parish have a great love of this Irishman whom fate
chose to lay at rest in their care. Percy was no stranger to
Formby, where he made many friends and some of them
became the proud possessors of his paintings and other
artwork. Although it is almost eighty years since the
death of Percy French, fresh flowers can often be found
on his grave in the grounds of St. Lukes Parish Church, at
Formby in the north of Liverpool. It is doubtful if a more
pleasant setting could be found for the remains of Percy
French. On his birthday, the 1 May, each year the
congregation of the Parish of St. Lukes honour the
memory of Percy French with a little service at his
graveside. The grave is so well attended it can give the
impression that internment had taken place in recent
times, his headstone reads:

'In Memory Of A Well Loved Song Writer, Poet Painter,
Author-Entertainer,
AR DHEIS DE GO RAIBH A ANEM AMEN.
William Percy French, Born At Clooniquin Co
Rosscommon, May 1st 1854.
Died at Formby Jan 24th 1920.
So Long The Power Hath Blest Me Sure It Still Will Lead
Me On.
OE'R MOOR AND FEN OE'R CRAG AND TORRANT
TILL THE NIGHT IS GONE.'

Members of the Liverpool Irish Centre added a block of Mourne Granite to the headstone on the fiftieth anniversary of his death, which reads:

'This Plinth of Mourne Granite Was Placed by the Irish Centre of Liverpool on behalf of a Grateful Nation on 24th Jan 1970 the 50th Anniversary of the death of Percy French.'

The songs of Percy French still linger on and have been recorded by several Irish singers in recent years. That lovely song 'The Mountains of Mourne', was always a favorite in Liverpool and who could forget,

'Come Back Paddy Reilly',
'Phil the Fluter's Ball',
'Are Ye Right There, Michael'
'Eileen Oge and Gortnamona'.

Every few years the parish Church of St. Luke, have 'An Evening with Percy French', in the Parish Hall. In many ways we must be thankful that we have artists like the late, Brendan O'Dowda and John Roche who made it their life's work to sing the songs of Percy French. There are also two books available on his with reference, in them to the St. Luke's connection, 'A Picture of Percy French' by Alan Tonge and 'The World of Percy French' by Brendan O'Dowda.

14

James William Carling
Artist

James Carling

People living in the Vauxhall and Scotland Road area of Liverpool today, or indeed those who have moved away over the years to settle in other parts of Merseyside, may not have heard of James Carling. He was born in 1857 in Addison Street, in an area that was known as the Irish quarter, a town within a town, which made up one-third of the population of Liverpool. He was the son of a blacking maker Henry Carling, his mother being Rose and he was the youngest of their six children. Catherine was the eldest born in London, and the next two sons William and John were born in Hull, Yorkshire. The younger of the children, Henry, Terence and James were born in Liverpool. In the 1861 census there was a married couple Terence and Ann Jane Lynch living with the Carling family at 38 Addison Street. It is possible Terence was the brother of Rose Carling.

Living at 38 Addison Street in 1861
Henry Carling 33 years, born Hull
Rose Carling 33 years, born Ireland
Catherine Carling 15 years, born London
William Carling 11 years, born Hull
John Carling 9 years, born Hull
Henry Carling 7 years, born Liverpool
Terence Carling 5 years, born Liverpool
James Carling 3 years, born Liverpool
Terence Lynch 40 years, born Ireland
Ann Jane Lynch 40 years, born Ireland

James Carling was known as the 'little artist' later, as 'little chalky', and began his career on the pavements of Liverpool.

Sadly James and the other siblings lost their mother Rose when she was thirty-six, and, James the youngest child was only seven years of age. His father married a widow whom James remembered with some bitterness, for when he was grown up he wrote:

> Starved by a stepmother of a very unusual disposition, I sallied out into the world like Jack of the fairy tales to seek my fortune, and a living as well, at the ripe old age of five.

James and his brothers earned pennies as errand boys and as a result of singing at English parish festivals, he could also quote Shakespeare and other poets. He learned the classics at an early age, and with his brothers were in regular attendance at Liverpool's theatres, gaining admission to the 'gods' for pennies. He remembered playing at Liverpool's Pierhead on a Sunday morning and listening to the chimes of the Anglican St. Nicholas Church.

James and his brothers, Willy, Johnny and Henry had gone onto the streets at an early age as pavement artists. In their boyish ways they became political lampooners of the municipal government and were the delight of newsboys and street performers (buskers). But the pavement artists were the kings of the street Arabs, (neglected or homeless boys or girls). The police were no friends of theirs as they drove them off the streets in continuing warfare, but there were too many homeless and hungry children for the police to keep full control. The Carling boys were big for their years in a town where many poor children had stunted growth through lack of proper nourishment. One of James memories was of a brutal struggle between his brother Johnny and a peeler (policeman) who clubbed the boy mercilessly.

Five-year-old James Carling, who had observed his older brothers practising their street art, was given his chance to follow in their footsteps by Johnny when he gave him some paints and crayons. Early the following morning James made his way to Ranelagh Street in the town centre to claim the most suitable smooth flagstone to practice his art. His subjects that morning, were the prizefighters, English champion Tom Sayers and Irish American champion John C. Heenan. Passers by were so amused by the talent of one so young they started throwing coins into his little upturned hat and this encouragement drove him on.

The streets of Liverpool were now the studio of little James Carling and the flagstones the canvas on which to display his works of art. James accepted guidance from his older brothers who were also street artists and he soon became well known, among other children and passers by. Unlike most of the street artists in the town he did not draw the same picture twice. Working his drawings onto the pavement had its pitfalls, as on rainy days the rain could wash his enterprise away. At other times a policeman would beat him if he tried to practice his art on the streets used by the gentry.

Eventually James found the right spot on rainy days, under an arcade at the bottom of James Street, just a few hundred yards (metres) from where Liverpool's Liver Building would be built many years later. This was not a good place to catch the eye of the wealthy toffs to throw a few coppers into the hat as most of his admirers were working men who had little or no money. They admired the young James who could produce such fine artwork on a paving stone. In return they would supply him with cockles, shrimps and periwinkles, or any other food they might have on them. Seamen were amongst his most generous benefactors and some days he would collect up to two shillings a day off them.

Lime Street was another of his favourite thoroughfares; here was a never-ending flow of people of every shape and size. From the well-heeled, with their expensive attire, to the tramp with his battered boots, it was a shifting open theatre, a carousel that changed with the blink of an eye, of minstrels and acrobats, of bootblacks and pavement artists.

James Carling never forgot his boyhood on the streets of Liverpool. He would often recall his time spent in Ranelagh Street which was not free of policemen, who would often beat him although he was only six years of age:

"I knew I was too small to be incarcerated, for I was often arrested for drawing sidewalk pictures and taking their brutal beatings as a matter of course. I drew my pictures, preferring a bloody face and a bruised limb to inanition (exhaustion from want of food) and death by starvation". James carried through life the contempt he felt for the well-heeled people of the town "Bold Street! My heart sickens at your name. And well it might, for I not only could not draw in that street I could not walk on it. The sight of a ragged coat was enough to bring the harsh, 'move on' or what was worse, the most brutal application of the staff. On Bold Street, promenade of the local aristocracy, the Gocking (pavement artist) did not draw."

On Christmas Eve, 1865, James had just reached his eighth birthday and made his way to Elliot Street to make some money for Christmas. It was a cold day and the biting wind was eating into his frail young body. As the day went on, he made his way to Lime Street, and no sooner had the young pavement artist started working than he felt the hands of a policeman as he was jerked to his feet. The young James Carling was dragged off to Cheapside Jail in the heart of the town.

He spent Christmas Eve in a police cell, then on Christmas Day he was transferred to the community workhouse for a week. It was then decided, that James William Carling be ordered to spend six years in St. George's Industrial School. The Headmaster at St. George's was Father Nugent a man who cared about the welfare of his young charges. The six years in the care of Father Nugent and his staff gave James Carling the opportunity to learn to read and write and the ability to express himself. James in later life never forgot what the school and Father Nugent did for him and when he returned to his school for a visit he was shown around by his old headmaster. A statue to Father Nugent, with his hand on the head of a young boy, stands in St. John's Gardens, William Brown Street Liverpool.

James was released from Father Nugent's Industrial School at the age of fourteen. His older brother Henry then took him to Philadelphia, in the United States of America, where they renewed their careers as sidewalk artists. A newspaperman took an interest in James and he became the subject of a feature story. The manager of a vaudeville troupe saw the article and contacted him to appear as the troupe's Lightning Caricaturist. James later performed in a New York musical spectacular called, 'The Black Crook' where he appeared as a popular chalk talk performer. The show took the young James all over America and during this time the boy from Liverpool was perfecting his art. After six years on the road with the musical spectacular, he joined his brother Henry in Chicago, where the latter had established a studio.

It was in Chicago, at the age of twenty-three, that James went in for a competition in 'Harper's Magazine' for illustrations for a special gift edition of 'The Raven' a poem by Edgar Allen Poe. He entered thirty-three of the forty-three illustrations he had done in his brother's studio in Chicago. However in 1883 Harper's magazine announced to the world the winner of their competition. To illustrate "The most magnificent book of the year and in many cardinal particulars the most superb volume that has ever issued from the press of this or any other country the stately and luxurious folio, 'The Raven' was by Gustave Dore". He was a specialist in the bizarre and fantastic, whose editions of 'Paradise Lost', 'Divine Comedy', 'the Bible', the works of Balzac and other classic and contemporary works had made him the most popular and internationally famous illustrator of his century.

Fate had delivered a hammer blow to James Carling when it snatched away his chance to walk in the sun and leave behind the cold pavements of Liverpool. George F. Sheer in his research on James Carling wrote: "He returned to Europe, probably at this time to collect his grandfather's songs and ballads. He returned to Liverpool in the spring of 1887 with the intention of studying at the National School of Art". It is doubtful, however, that he even entered the school, for by the summer, James Carling became ill and according to the Brownlow Hill Workhouse Admission Records he was:

Admitted 17 June 1887
James Carling 29
Place of settlement Liverpool
Religion: R. C.
Trade or calling, Artist
Condition: Single
Name of relations, no friends
Where slept last night, 94 Fontenoy Street
Date of death 9 July 1887

James Carling like so many great artists died young, at just twenty-nine, he was so poor and unknown that he was buried along with 15 others in 1887 near the demure little chapel at Walton Park, in what was then called the

Liverpool Parish Cemetery. The grave was registered Section F, Grave 16, but no one raised a marker of any kind until 1984.

James Carling's eldest brother Henry Carling made a successful career for himself and settled in Minnesota in the United States. He won membership of the Beaux-Arts of Paris and the Royal Academy of Liverpool. It was Henry Carling who kept the memory of his brother alive by looking after his drawings. In 1930 when Henry was seventy-four years of age he gave an exhibition of his own work and hung several of the 'The Raven' drawings with his own. The works of James Carling were once again stored away, but six years later, following the death of Henry, his daughter Stella took on the job of promoting the work of her uncle James. Stella was determined to find a fitting place for these illustrations of Poe's poem. They were lent to the Poe Shrine in Richmond, Virginia, for the Edgar Allen Poe memorial week in 1936, where they can still be seen

In September 1984, Walton Park cemetery was the scene of an unveiling ceremony when the grave of the forgotten Liverpool artist was marked. Members of the Rice Lane Community Association, Liverpool, worked long and hard to uncover Carling's history and produced the simple grave monument. The ceremony was carried out by Dr. Roscoe Brown Fisher of North Carolina, author of the book "The James Carling Illustrations of Edgar Allen Poe's 'The Raven'.

Addison Street one of Carling's street scenes.

Addison Street 1924.

15

Lucy Cometina Kurtz
and
Douglas Hyde

The name Lucy Cometina Kurtz will not come readily to most people's minds, but the name of Douglas Hyde, first President of the Republic of Ireland 1938-1945, will be familiar to many. In 1891-93 Douglas was teaching languages at the University of New Brunswick, Canada, and it was during this period that he met Lucy Kurtz.

Lucy was born in 1861 and christened in the Church of St. Peter, in Church Street, Liverpool. The church was demolished some time in the 1920s to make way for a group of shops. Set into the pavement in front of the shops is a Maltese cross, on the spot were the Church of St. Peter stood. Lucy lived in Burbo Bank Road, the very fashionable area of Blundellsands on Merseyside,

At the time of her marriage to Douglas Hyde in St. Nicholas Church, Blundellsands, their marriage certificate shows that on the 10th October 1893 Douglas Hyde married Lucy Cometina Kurtz. Douglas Hyde was living in French Park, County Roscommon, age 32, Bachelor, Doctor of Laws, father Arthur Hyde, Clerk in Holy Orders. Lucy Cometina Kurtz, age 32 Spinster, lived in Blundellsands, father Charles Kurtz deceased, Manufacturer. They were married in the presence of Charles George Kurtz and Agnes Green. Douglas and Lucy had two daughters Mary Una and Nuala Eileen.

Lucy's father Charles Kurtz, was born about 1812 in Odessa Russia and became a Naturalised British Subject. He was descended from Mattau Kurtz who was ennobled by the Emperor Karl V in 1540. Charles was a Manufacturing Chemist and Tar Distiller with a number of premises in Liverpool. Her mother was Lucy Charlotte

Kurtz, born about 1833 in the Danish West Indies, at St. Croix (now the US Virgin Islands) and her maiden name was Hill. She married Charles Kurtz when she was aged 27 in 1861, and was his second wife. He had three children from his former marriage, and was aged 69. His daughter, also Lucy, was born in 1861 and she went on to marry Douglas Hyde in 1893. Lucy spent the first 32 years of her life in Liverpool and Llanrwst North Wales. They set up home in Ratra Frenchpark, County Roscommon which was also his birthplace.

Douglas Hyde was born 17 January 1860 in French Park, County Roscommon, his father Arthur Hyde was the local Church of Ireland rector. As a young man he became fascinated with hearing the old people in the locality speaking the Irish language, which was looked down on at the time by many and seen as backward and old fashioned.

To please his father he read divinity and graduated with distinction but he had no taste for a clerical life so did not follower a career in the church. Douglas instead became an academic. He entered Trinity College, Dublin, where he became fluent in French, Latin, German, Greek and Hebrew. He went back to Trinity to study Law and graduated with a doctorate. He taught languages at the University of New Brunswick, Canada 1891-93.

He had a varied career as an academic after his marriage and involved himself in preservation of the Irish language and the fostering of the Gaelic League. His passion for Irish, led him to found the Gaelic league, Conradh na Gaeilge, in the hope of saving his native language from extinction. This Irish Language Movement, initially seen as eccentric, gained a mass following throughout Ireland. Douglas published a pamphlet called 'The Necessity for De-Anglicising Ireland', arguing that Ireland should follow her own traditions in language and literature. In 1909, he accepted the post of professor of Modern Irish at the National University of Ireland, 1909-32. Douglas gave his support to William Butler Yeats, Lady Gregory and

J. M. Synge and others in promoting Irish culture, culminating in the opening of Ireland's first national theatre the Abbey Theatre, in Lower Abbey Street.

At the age of 78 years Douglas was plucked from retirement by Taoiseach, Eamon de Valera and asked to stand for the position of President of Ireland. By 1938 Ireland had ceased to be a Free State and had become a Republic, so Douglas Hyde became first President of the new Republic of Ireland. While still President, Douglas and King George V1 (who was still legally King of Ireland and would remain so until 1 April 1949) corresponded about stamp collecting.

Douglas Hyde is notable in that he is the only leader of independent Ireland to be featured on its bank notes. With his handlebar moustache and warm personality he was a popular President. United States President Franklin D. Roosevelt, called President Hyde a 'fine old gentleman'. Sadly Lucy was not by her husband's side when he was appointed President of Ireland as she died on 31 December 1937 at Ratra in French Park, County Roscommon. In April 1940, Douglas suffered a massive stroke.

Plans were made for his lying-in-state and state funeral but to the surprise of everyone he survived to see out his Presidency in 1945, and died quietly on 12th July 1949. As a former President he was accorded a state funeral and the service took place in Church of Ireland, St. Patrick's Cathedral. Attending the funeral was Eamon de Valera and Erskine Childers who was to become President of Ireland in 1973-74, Douglas was buried in his native Roscommon close to his father's old church, which is now a museum, dedicated to showing memorabilia of President Hyde.

Some regard Douglas as the Anglican squire who took up the cause of the Irish language and ended up as the first President of Ireland, but he was much more than that he was a true and patriotic Irishman. The Church of St. Nicholas is a High Church of England and the congregation are very proud of the fact that the man who would become President of Ireland married one of their own. Just recently the Church Newsletter carried a little article about that momentous occasion when Douglas Hyde and Lucy Kurtz took their wedding vows in the Church.

16

Dame May Whitty

-----May, with her built-in Irish passion for being "agin" the government", found herself becoming eloquent in defence of women's rights.

Margaret Webster

Many children over the years will have seen May Whitty, granddaughter of 'Michael James Whitty' she was the kindly farmer's wife on television in the film 'Lassie Come Home' first released in 1951. In her first talking film, 'Night Must Fall', shown in 1937, May played the part of a foolhardy lady who falls for the charms of homicidal Robert Montgomery.

Dame May Whitty, was born Mary Louise Whitty on June 19th 1865 in Liverpool. Her father was Alfred Whitty the youngest son of Michael James Whitty, the newspaper proprietor. Alfred married Mary Aston, a Lancashire woman, and they had three children, May being the youngest. The young May Whitty was adventurous and determined and had the same discipline for detail as her grandfather Michael James Whitty but her love of the theatre came from her father Alfred.

He was a gregarious man, loving music and the

theatre. He lost a lot of money collaborating with Henry James Byron, the dramatist, on the management of the Court Theatre, Liverpool. May first appeared on stage at the age of sixteen, unrehearsed in the chorus-line playing the part of a sylph in the 'Mountain Sylph', at the Court Theatre Liverpool. A year later, still in the chorus line, she made her first appearance on the London stage on April 11th, 1882 in the operetta 'La Mascotte'. After eighteen months, and still in the chorus line, May took steps to change direction. She wanted to be an actress and that would never happen while she was thus employed. She applied to the St. James Theatre for an audition and much to her surprise was accepted.

May stayed at the St. James for two years understudying for the well-established actors, and playing small parts while learning her craft. However she felt the days of playing the understudy had come to an end and it was time to strike out on her own. She was determined to become a leading actress. Her chance came when she joined a touring company and played two weeks in Edmonton, London with short tours of the small halls. They did twelve plays and May took the lead in eleven of them in parts such as Lady Teazle, Lydia Languish and Kate, and with the plays 'The Shaughraun' and 'East Lyne'. She made a good impression as Susan Throssell in Barrie's, 'Quality Street' at the Vaudeville Theatre and was in constant demand in the West End, appearing in such successes as 'Trelawny of the Wells' and 'The Madras House'. May married Ben Webster in 1892, in London and they had one child, Margaret. Ben was from an acting background and educated at Stationers' School and King's College, Cambridge. He was a barrister but chose the theatre for his living, making his debut in 1887 in the play 'Clancarty'. Ben and May lived for years in a flat in Bedford Street, Covent Garden. Their London home was a meeting place for English and American actors and was always a refuge and a comfort for those in trouble.

May did not confine her energies to acting alone, and

had many other interests. One of those was the Theatrical Ladies' Guild and her diary records attendance at a meeting as early as 1892. The organization had been formed to help all distressed members of the profession, actors, stagehands, wardrobe mistresses, anyone in need. The organisation hated the word charity and abhorred red tape. It took care of children, paid doctors' bills, provided coal and blankets in winter, and dispensed such items as spectacles and dentures. May became a member of the committee and later she was, for many years, chairman.

May was drawn into other similar organizations including the Actors' Orphanage, with its famous annual garden party, and the Three Arts Club, with its equally renowned annual ball. May arranged innumerable benefits, made vast quantities of appeals, and sat on many committees and invariably gravitated toward the Chair.

She was drawn into the Women's Suffrage movement and in 1908 attended a meeting to hear Mrs. Pankhurst who spoke about all the concerns May already had, including the struggle for women to enter the professions, to become qualified doctors, lawyers and teachers. Even in the theatre they were only recognized as actresses, but certainly not as stage managers, directors, nor managers. One woman to break through such taboos was Annie Horniman a founder of the Abbey Theatre Dublin and of the Gaiety Theatre, Manchester. Margaret Webster in her biography, 'The Same Only Different' wrote:

> May, with her built-in Irish passion for being "agin' the government", found herself becoming eloquent in defense of women's rights. At last, one of her friends remarked jokingly: "Why, May, I believe you're a suffragette"! May paused, slightly astonished. "Why", she said, "I believe I am".

In Dublin, in 1899, May Whitty played the part of Countess Cathleen in the play of the same name, by William Butler Yeats and Maud Gonne attended the first night. May had been one of the leading lights of the British stage for nearly twenty-five years when she appeared in her first film, 'Enoch Arden', in 1914, but caring little for the experience she made only a few silent films. In 1918 the fifty-three year old May had the distinction of being the first actress to be created a Dame Commander of the British Empire in recognition of her above-and-beyond activities performed before the troops in World War 1. May had a succession of Broadway successes, and then she and Ben took themselves off to Hollywood to live there for the remainder of their lives. Some of the films May appeared in were.

The Lady Vanishes
Conquest
Raffles, Bill of Divorcement
Suspicion
For Ever and a Day
The Constant Nymph
Lassie Come Home
Flesh and Fantasy
Madam Currie
The White Cliffs of Dover
Gas Light
My Name is Julia Ross
Devotion
Green Dolphin Street
If Winter Comes
The Return of October

May's daughter Margaret Webster, born in New York City, was an American actress, producer and director. Margaret Webster tells the story of meeting Elizabeth Bowen, Dennis Johnson and Padraic Colum at a symposium in 1952, on 'The Irish Theatre'.

Mr. Colum, they told me, was the self-effacing little man in the corner of the Faculty Lounge, where I was being given tea. I got myself introduced to him. I told him that I hated having to miss the symposium, but I was lecturing myself that evening. "I'm particularly interested", I said, "because my mother played 'The Countess Cathleen' in the special performance when Yeats and Lady Gregory inaugurated what afterward became the 'Abbey Theatre'. He was very faintly interested and asked her name. "May Whitty", I replied. He disapproved. "It's not an Irish name". I bristled somewhat. "There are records of the Whitty's in County Wexford in the twelfth century; sometimes sheriffs and sometimes horse thieves; but there". "Oh", he answered, nonchalant but firm, "they may have come over with the Normans, but they're not Irish". I could hear the ghost of Michael James Whitty come screaming over the white-pillared portico calling upon his great-granddaughter to do something with fire and sword.

Ben Webster died in Los Angeles 26th February 1947. Dame May Whitty died the following year, 29 May 1948, also in Los Angeles.

17

James and Delia Larkin

In 1980, RTE Television produced a drama 'Strumpet City' adapted for the screen from the book of the same name, by James Plunkett Kelly. It tells the story of the destitute workers being locked out of their place of employment because of their need to join a trade union, in the hope that it would lift them out of their state of poverty because of low wages and long working hours. The story centres round the efforts of people like James Larkin born in Liverpool.

Liverpool is well known for producing those who fought for the working class, to have the right to decent pay and working conditions. The Larkin family produced not one but two such people in the form of James and Delia Larkin and Libraries of Merseyside hold reference to them. Jim was sent to Dublin from Liverpool by the 'Transport and General Workers Union' to organise the trade union movement in Ireland.

From 1907 he had built up the militant Irish Transport and General Workers Union. It catered primarily for unskilled and unorganised workers and it relied more especially upon the weapon of the lighting strike. In 1913, W. M. Murphy, the richest man in Dublin,

Chairman of the Employers' Federation, virtual owner of the Dublin Tramways and owner of the 'Independent Newspaper' denounced workers on strike in that journal. Larkin called a boycott of the 'Independent' and Murphy replied by calling for employers' to lock all members of the Transport Union from the Tramway Service and Jacob's Biscuit Factory, which he also controlled.

Opposite Clery's Department store in O'Connell Street Dublin, stands a statue of the great labour leader James Larkin. This is just a few metres away from where Larkin made a speech on August 31st 1913, rallying thousands of workers, who had been locked out of their place of employment for being members of trade unions. Larkin called a protest meeting, which the authorities promptly banned. Larkin said he would be there "dead or alive".

At the prescribed time of the meeting Larkin made his way into the Imperial Hotel owned by William Martin Murphy, and heavily disguised, he made his way onto the balcony of the hotel. From here he immediately began to speak to the assembled crowd, as police hidden inside streets erupted into a charge with batons drawn. Hundreds of unarmed people who had no notion of attending a meeting were mercilessly clubbed and many of them ended up in hospital. Scarcely had the lockout of workers from their places of employment begun when a new weekly newspaper appeared in Dublin. Its title was 'The Toiler' and its purpose was to attack Larkin and his colleagues. C. Desmond Greaves, editor of the 'Irish Democrat' newspaper, gives an insight into the character of the editor of 'The Toiler':

> Its editor was one McIntyre, Wexford born son of a landlord's agent, he specialised in personal vilification. McIntyre made two charges against Larkin's lineage. First that he was the son of the notorious informer Carey, secondly he was the son of a Liverpool Orangeman. Not satisfied with that he then accused Larkin of being married to the daughter of a prominent Liverpool man. Larkin did not reply,

perhaps this was merely to refuse to submit to blackmail. 'The London Times' remarked that Larkin was under no obligation to disclose particulars of his upbringing in order to satisfy Mr. McIntyre's curiosity. But undoubtedly Larkin was hard pressed at some of his meetings when members of the Redmondite party (United Irish Party) would wave copies of 'The Toiler', and ask him to refute its allegations.

Transport Union members fought the people brought in to run the Tramways and newsboys did likewise with the sellers that Murphy sent out with the 'Independent'. Other workers joined in, railwaymen, transport-drivers, dockers and seamen all refused to handle Jacob's Biscuits or the goods of any of the firms who joined in Murphy's war against Larkin and the Transport Union. Soon half of Dublin was on strike and all Dublin was in an uproar as battles with the police were fought daily.

The working class were faced with an alliance of Dublin Castle (with its police), the Orange-Tory magistrates, the Nationalist employers and the Catholic Hierarchy. Larkin turned to England and Scotland from which they received a burst of enthusiastic solidarity such as not been seen since the great dockers' strike of 1888. Virtually every union granted funds, by the TUC, the Labour Party and the Co-operative Union. Jacob's Biscuits were universally boycotted and the Trade Unions and socialist societies combined to stock a food-ship, which the C.W.S. supplied at cost price, chartering the ship as their share. English and Scottish socialists volunteered by the hundred to find homes for the children of strikers "for the duration".

A party of some three hundred children was actually on its way to the ship at the North Wall Docks, Dublin, when it was turned back by a frenzied band of hymn-singing women, headed by priests, who feared the consequences to the children's souls if they were fed for a month or so in the homes of 'Godless' English and Scottish socialists.

James Larkin left Ireland for America in October 1914. In 1919 he was put on trial in the U.S.A. on the strange charge of "criminal Anarchy" He had helped to organise a break away from the Socialist Party of America called the 'Communist Labour Party'. Evidence that he was a bad character was supplied by the American consul in Dublin, and this was backed up by a birth certificate purporting to show that he was born in Liverpool on May 2nd 1879. Desmond Greaves wrote. "I confess that I found the same entry at St. Catherine's House and that it took me in for a time". Larkin has had two biographers, R. M. Fox who published his work in 1955 and Emmett Larkin, who produced his more ambitious work in 1965. But Larkin's is really the earlier work. For it was written in the early fifties as a post-graduate thesis. Desmond Greaves wrote:

There are moreover important particulars in Fox that are absent from Emmett Larkin. Fox and Emmett Larkin agree that the birthplace was Liverpool. Both give the year as 1876. Emmett Larkin gives a precise date, January 21st but he cannot have searched the register of births. I was unable to find any such entry myself, and I have a letter from the registrar in Liverpool saying that he cannot find any such entry in that city. So we must turn to the incidental information provided by Fox who had the journalist's nose for significant detail.

Fox says that Larkin's father James Larkin married Mary McNulty. This is of tremendous importance. He says that the family were settled in Liverpool and that James', father Bernard joined them when he lost his farm in the north of Ireland. Fox says James was the youngest son and that his brothers were named Bernard, Hugh and Patrick, he had two sisters Margaret and Delia. James attended Chipping Street School and Our Lady of Mount Carmel.

Marie McQuade, Liverpool family history researcher,

found the parents of James and Delia Larkin in the 1871 census and that James Larkin and Mary Ann McNulty were married on the 24 July 1871 at St Patrick's, Liverpool. They were living at 3 house, 42 Court Henderson Street. The 1881 census finds James and Mary Ann Larkin living at 6 house, 4 Court, Prophet Street, Toxteth Park.

James Larkin, 31 years of age, head of household, labourer in foundry born in Ireland
Mary Ann Larkin 32 years of age, wife born in Ireland
Hughey son 8 years of age scholar born Liverpool
James son 7 years of age scholar born Liverpool
Bridget (Delia) daughter 3 years of age born Liverpool
Peter, son 8 months born Liverpool.

Jim Larkin's grandson gives many examples of Jim Larkin's birthplace, in his family biography 'In The Footsteps of Big Jim' published by Blackwater Press. He informs his readers that Big Jim was born in Tamnaharry County Down in 1876. This date does not correspond with the 1881 census, giving James Larkin's age at 7 years, born in Liverpool, so 1874 appears to be the year of his birth. The details on the 1881 census would have been given by the parents of James Larkin.

There appears to be no doubt as to the birthplace of Delia Larkin. Born the 27th of February 1878 at home in 2 Court Fermie Street, in the Toxeth Park district of Liverpool and baptised at Our Lady of Mount Carmel R.C. She attended the Chipping Street elementary school and was confirmed in Our Lady of Mount Carmel where she had been baptised. Her given name was Bridget and her confirmation name was Mary.

She was the fifth child and eldest surviving daughter, of Mary Ann Larkin and James Larkin. An older sister, Agnes had died in infancy. Her father James died in 1887 when she was nine, so her oldest brothers, Hugh and James, had to support their widowed mother. Delia Larkin started work early to help her brothers so her schooling was cut short. Delia had an interest in literature and social politics from an early age (possibly fuelled by James Larkin's interests).

Delia Larkin's first official record in Ireland is the census of 1911 when she is listed as living with her older brother James and his family at 27 Auburn Street, near Broadstone Dublin. She is known to have a nursing career in Liverpool before her trade union appointment but her occupation given (in Irish) on the census form is teacher. Not much is known of her life except it is thought she ran a hotel in Rostrevor, Co Down, about the time James Larkin was an official for the National Union of Dock Labourers, and strike leader in Belfast in 1907.

Delia Larkin first became involved in the trade union movement in the summer of 1911. It was decided to start a union for women within the Irish Transport and General Workers Union (the union formed by James Larkin) called the Irish Woman Workers Union (IWWU). The union first advertised for members in the 'Irish Worker' on the 12th of August 1911 and was launched formally a month later on the 5th of September. Delia Larkin wrote an article in the 'Irish Worker' the weekly paper for the Irish Transport and General Workers Union summing up the aspirations of the new union. "All we ask for is just shorter hours, better pay than the scandalous limit now existing and conditions of labour befitting a human being".

Her column dealt with many different issues such as housing, social conditions and votes for women. The aim of the union was to provide women with a union, which widened opportunities and broke down barriers to allow them to form different backgrounds and to mix on equal terms. The union programme included discussion groups and weekly socials, annual outings, yearly concerts and New Year dances. Within the first six months £170 had been paid out in strike pay, and the union won £7 a week increase in wages. They were largely Dublin based, although branches were also set up in Belfast, Dundalk, Wexford and Cork. Delia represented her union at three annual conferences of the Irish Trade Union Council from

1912 to 1914. She also represented women on Ireland's first Trades Board, the joint industrial council formed to regulate pay within the poorly paid manufacturing sectors where women worked.

Along with her industrial activity Delia also formed the union choir in February 1912 and this was to lead on to the formation of a drama group four months later, Delia Larkin also represented the union's members within the suffragette movement.

Within weeks of the Dublin Tram strike starting at the end of August 1913, it had spread throughout the city. The lockout paralysed the city and threw thousands out of work. At Jacob's the dispute began on 1, September over the wearing of the Irish Women's Workers Union badge. Within a week 310 women were locked out and Delia Larkin took effective charge in Liberty Hall. She formed and ran the entire undertaking to feed the union members and their dependants throughout the lockout.

This huge effort provided daily breakfast for three thousand children, lunches for nursing mothers, and the distribution of clothing, continued until February 1914. When the 'Daily Herald' league planned to bring Dublin striker's children to homes in Britain for care during the lockout, the London organisers turned to Delia Larkin for support with the arrangements. The lockout ended in the early months of 1914, although this provided little relief from the pressure of Delia Larkin's commitments in the coming year. Four hundred of her union members were thus not reinstated. It is believed Delia went in 1914, to war-torn Liverpool in order to work as a nurse, and returned to Dublin at the end of hostilities in 1918.

Delia married Patrick Colgan, a member of the Citizen Army and they lived in a flat at 17 Gardner Street. After 1924 Delia renewed her theatrical activities with members of the Workers' Union of Ireland. During the years 1930 to 1931 Delia wrote occasional pieces for the relaunched 'Irish Worker'. When Delia and Patrick Colgan moved to Ballsbridge Dublin, James Larkin joined them and lived out his last years in their flat at 41

Wellington Road Dublin. In the final years of her life Delia suffered from ill health, which caused "a very quiet life, quiet against my inclination", as she said in a letter to R. M. Fox shortly after the death of James Larkin in January 1947. Delia died at her home, 41 Wellington Road, Dublin, on the 26 October 1949 and was buried at Glasnevin Cemetery.

James Larkin, statue on O'Connell Street, Dublin

18

Robert Noonan

---A few months ago a friend asked me to look at the manuscript of a novel, 'The Ragged Trousered Philanthropists,' the work of a socialistic house painter, who wrote his book and died. I consented without enthusiasm, expecting to be neither interested nor amused---and found I had chanced upon a remarkable human document.

Jessie Pope

In 1914 the Richards Press under the name of Robert Tressell published 'The Ragged Trousered Philanthropists'. Thus was the pseudonym of Robert Noonan, an Irish housepainter, who came to England from South Africa at the beginning of the twentieth century. His daughter Kathleen and sister Adelaide accompanied him. They settled in Hastings, Sussex, where he worked as a signwriter for various building firms.

The Ragged Trousered Philanthropists' was the story of a group of building workers and the conditions in which they toiled, it portrayed the life of the common man before the First World War. The main character of the novel is Owen, who tries to enlighten his workmates but they refuse to listen, so he calls them philanthropists because they exchange their skills for little reward. Such was the impact of this novel, that between April 1914 and November 1949 it was reprinted twenty times.

Almost thirty years had gone by after its first printing, when a man living in Hastings, Fred Ball, read the novel and was surprised to see the book was set in his town. (Hastings is referred to as Mugsborough in the book.) Fred Ball decided to research information on the author of the novel that so fascinated him. He found, much to his surprise, that Robert Tressell was the pen name of Robert Noonan, a Dublin man. Robert was born in Dublin on the 18 April 1870, at 37 Wexford Street, His father Samuel was an inspector in the Royal Irish Constabulary and later a magistrate. Samuel had three daughters and one son to Robert's mother and three sons from a previous marriage. When Robert was just five or six his father died and this had a lasting effect on him, as he had been attached to him. Robert's sisters were educated at a convent in Dublin, but Robert missed out on a decent education. A few years later his mother married again, a marriage that Robert never approved of and he never got on with his stepfather.

Robert appears to have left Dublin for England when he was quite young, possibly in his teens. In 1890, Robert decided to chance his luck in South Africa. He could not have been there very long when he met his future wife. On the 15th October 1891 Robert married Elizabeth Hartel, age 18 at a Protestant church in Cape Town and on the 17th September 1892 his daughter Kathleen was born in Cape Town. Kathleen was baptized at a Protestant Church and in April, 1895 Elizabeth died of typhoid fever. In August 1896 Robert and his young daughter Kathleen moved to Johannesburg, this brought him into contact with John McBride, the leader of "The Irish Brigade" which fought on the side of the Boers against the British in South Africa.

Mr Ogilvy, a friend of Robert's said. "His literary

talent was in evidence during his time in South Africa, he was very fond of writing and wrote for various publications and his publications gave ample evidence of his literary power". In 1898, Robert's sister Adelaide joined him in South Africa with her young son Arthur, after the death of her husband in Chile. In September 1901 Robert, his sister and the two children, Kathleen and Arthur sailed to England, on the Steam Ship Galician. The four of them joined his sister Mary Jane, at 38 Western Road, St Leonards.

Much of Robert's early life is shrouded in mystery and those who knew him after his return from South Africa with Kathleen were never privileged to learn of this very private man's past. Someone who had worked with Robert said he was one of the best sign writers he had known and would have made a brilliant artist. Robert soon found accommodation for himself and his widowed sister and the two children, which was a top flat in Grosvenor Mansion, 115 Milward Rd St, Hastings. Kathleen was sent to the Roman Catholic School, the Convent of the Sacred Heart in Old London Rd.

In South Africa, Robert had put his skills in sign writing to full use enabling him to be his own master as a self-employed man. Robert soon found work after his return home at a time when jobs in his trade were easy to come by, with Bruce & Co, Electrical, Sanitary Engineers, and Builders. His skills were soon rewarded with a pay increase, as a first class interior decorator and signwriter. Sadly this well paid employment came to an end when Bruce and Co, went out of business but Robert, soon found work with Burton & Co, Builders Contractors and Funeral Directors. Throughout this unsettled period in his life Robert never ceased writing, despite the long hours of work.

There is no evidence as to when Robert started his novel, but Fred Ball thought that it may have been after he settled into his home in Hastings and based 'The Ragged Trousered Philanthropist' on his workmates. Working conditions in the building trade were not very pleasant, the long hours and the high volume of lead in the paint that Robert used every day seemed to bring about deterioration in his health. He was suffering increasing sickness, which in 1910 reduced him to real poverty.

Despite his illness Robert finished his manuscript of 1700 pages, all hand-written and this was sent to three publishers, who all returned it. The disappointment in having his manuscript rejected and his worsening health convinced him he could improve his lot in life by emmigrating to Canada and he made arrangements to go via Liverpool. Kathleen was now sixteen and it was decided she should stay with another aunt for a few weeks while Robert needed to earn the fare for himself and Kathleen and also sort things out with the Canadian Emigration authorities in Liverpool.

Kathleen never saw her father again. On the 3rd February 1911 Robert Noonan died at the age of forty in the Royal Liverpool Infirmary (workhouse hospital). The cause of death was bronchial pneumonia and he was buried in a pauper's grave, in Walton Cemetery. He never had the satisfaction and pleasure of seeing his book published. In 1914 Kathleen emigrated to Canada and married her cousin Paul Meiklejon. Her aunt, Mary Jane's daughter Kathleen, was believed to have been killed with her young daughter Joan in a car accident in 1918. However in June 1967 Fred Ball found Kathleen very much alive, aged seventy-five, living in Gloucestershire.

Fred Ball was like a ferret when it came to keeping the memory of Robert Noonan alive, as he found that the manuscript of 'The Ragged Troused Philanthropists' had been cut in half before publication in 1914. His determination to honour the memory of the Dublin man resulted in Lawrence and Wishart publishing the book in full in August 1958. In June 1967 BBC2 broadcast a dramatisation of Robert Tressell (Robert Noonan) and this was shown again in June 1969. But the interest in Robert Noonan did not stop there. 'The Times' published an interview with Kathleen, who by this time was seventy-seven and married to Reg Johnson and living in Gloucestershire.

Four years later in 1973 a memoir of Robert, by F.C. Ball 'One Of The Damned', was published. The memoir brings about renewed interest in Robert Noonan and a move to inaugurate a search was started to find his grave. John Nettleton, an admirer of the work of Robert Noonan led the way and the grave was found in Walton Cemetery, Liverpool, just a half a mile from the Infirmary were he died.

In 1977 a memorial stone was laid on Robert Noonan's grave, thanks mainly to John Nettleton. In April 1999 a plaque was placed on a building at the corner of 115 Milward Road and 88 Stonefield Road, Hastings. On 29th May 1999, Michael Foster, M.P. for Hastings & Rye, unveiled a blue plaque at 241 London Road, St. Leonards-on-Sea, as part of the Robert Tressell event. On 8th October 2000, Joan Johnson, Robert's granddaughter, born 7th November 1915 died at East Grinstead, Sussex, bringing an end to the last surviving relative of Robert Noonan.

19

Alderman
David Gilbert Logan, C.B.E., M.P.

On the death of Thomas Power O'Connor in 1929 a successor had to found to represent the people of the Scotland Division in Parliament. They did not have to look too far for the right person to represent them. This man was Alderman David Gilbert Logan, born on 22 November 1871, in 7 Court, Hornby Street in the Scotland Road area of Liverpool, to Thomas Logan (ship's cook) and Catherine McHugh, so he had an Irish mother and a Scots father.

In 1895 he married Susan, daughter of an engineer lost at sea on his first voyage. David Logan truly was a 'man of the people', born and reared among those he was about to represent in Parliament. For most of his life he lived at 362 Scotland Road, on the corner of Kew Street. On leaving school, David began work as a pawnbroker's assistant in a shop in Latimer Street, off Scotland Road, and later opened his own business in the same road. In 1912, he formed the National Pawnbrokers' Association

Approved Society and was its General Secretary for thirty-five-years until, in 1947, he handed over the administration of the society, (which by then had a membership of four-thousand,) to the State, according to the new National Insurance Act.

David Logan first attended St. Anthony's School and then St. Sylvester's after the parishes were extended. On a Saturday he delivered coal, to help with the family income. David may have left school at fourteen but his zest for learning did not end. After a day's work in a skittle alley, he studied the Greek philosophers, Plato, Socrates, and Diogenes. He read anything that would develop his understanding of life and help put an end to the poverty of barefoot women and children on Scotland Road. His early interest in politics was due to his mother's influence, as she was a supporter of T. P. O'Connor.

The young David Logan took an active part in the election of 1885 when T. P. O'Connor was elected to Parliament for the Scotland Division. Being a member of the 'Irish Nationalist League' was important to David Logan but an assembly meeting in Liverpool of Irish nationalists caused him to resign and join the Labour Party. Delegates present heard T. P. O'Connor declare that the assembly had come to an agreement in 1922 regarding the partition of Ireland. "I thought it was wrong", said David Logan.

> "We here have no right to decide on the partition of a nation without the vote of all the principal delegates of Great Britain. I move we call such a meeting for two weeks' time".
>
> "It can't be done," Tay Pay shouted back.
>
> "If it can't then this ends my association with the Irish Nationalist League and I will immediately join the Labour Party", was Logan's rejoinder.

The greater portion of the Irish Nationalists at that meeting followed David Logan into the Labour Party. Just before it selected a new candidate in 1929 to stand for the Scotland Division, Gray Quill of the 'Daily Post' wrote:

It needs a big man to occupy the place of T. P. O'Connor. As orator and writer we have none who can take his place. But, as the world's work must go on, there will be a new member representing Liverpool in Parliament, and, for the first time in its history, the Scotland Division will have a real member of Parliament who will come back to his home in the constituency every week, hear the grievances of the men and women who have returned him, and, to use his own phrase to me, "try to do nationally what I have been doing locally".

When the adoption meeting of Alderman David G. Logan, J.P. takes place tomorrow evening with the cream of the labour movement in Liverpool on the platform, the world outside Liverpool will realise that O'Connor will be succeeded in parliament by a man who has a fanatical hatred of the sordid poverty, which creates poverty, and the causes, which make it. There were two candidates from whom the executive committee of the Labour Party in the Scotland Division had to chose—both alderman of the City Council, David Logan and W. A. Robinson. And they rightfully selected a Scot-Irishman, the grandson of an Ayrshire man, a medical man who settled in Liverpool during the hungry forties of the last century, the son of an Irishwoman and a Liverpool Scot, who married an Irish School teacher, who gave him six children, a man from his earliest youth has been acquainted with the intense poverty caused by the accursed system of casual labour.

In his youth he was an apprentice to the pawn broking trade and in Athol Street he became painfully familiar with all the sordid tragedies of the poor. As a young man he was manager of several pawnshops which covered the area in which he has lived all his life, and has a first hand knowledge of the hand-to-mouth existence of the poor in Liverpool and elsewhere.

From some study of his character I have often thought that if there is such a thing as re-incarnation then David Logan is a modern incarnation of Don Quixote, the most lovable character in all fiction, whose sincerity gave rise to laughter first, tears afterwards and then lasting respect for the earnest effort of a man who was trying to make the world a better place than he found it, and often was misunderstood. He now steps on to a larger stage, with a fiercer limelight, and his appearance will be watched with critical, yet not unsympathetic eyes. He has to tell the story of a division of Parliament, where men and women marry early, beget children who have small outlook in life beyond the danger of the seas (and they have largely added to the story of the nation's heroism in this!), the fruitless ways of casual labour.

Alderman David Gilbert Logan was fifty-nine, when he filled the void Thomas Power O'Connor left in 1929. Most men of that age would have been thinking of retirement or moving their talents into something more pleasing to mind and body. The Conservatives did not bother to contest the seat for the Scotland Division, It being T. P. O'Connor', Kingdom for forty-four years. It was in 1920 when David was first elected to the Liverpool City Council as a representative of the South Scotland Ward. Nine years later, his fellow Councillors elected him an Alderman and he served the Council in this capacity for the rest of his life. During this period he was a member of the housing committee. In the same year that he became an Alderman, he was also elected Member of Parliament for the Scotland Division of Liverpool and he held this seat for the next thirty-five years until his death.

David Logan worked with unceasing vigour and energy for the people he represented, and among whom he lived, in Scotland Road. His door was always open to callers. He fought particularly to raise living standards and to defeat the scourge of unemployment. He told Gray Quill:

> I am going to Parliament to supplement the work of other labour men, with no thought of my own advancement, but solely with intense desire to serve my people! The broken soldier, the sailor who has been injured in the service of the country, whether of the Navy or the mercantile marine, the poor women who do not know, even now, with our twisted pension laws, whether they have a pension or not—in other words, the cause of the poor—all these I shall bear in mind when I get to Westminster. And the housing question—ah, there I can speak! I think that I shall be able to speak with some authority on the housing question and take my share in the work being done by the Labour Party.

His political and public services were recognised in 1949 when, in the New-Year's Honours' List, he was created a Commander of the Order of the British Empire. His devotion to his Church and his long public service, especially in the field of Roman Catholic education, was recognised by Pope Pius X11 in 1951 when he made Alderman Logan a Knight of St. Gregory the Great. The insignia of this Papal Knighthood was presented to Alderman Logan by the the Archbishop of Liverpool (Dr. Downey) at St. Anthony's School in Scotland Road.

David Logan died on the 25th February 1964, at the age of ninety years. At the time of his death, he was the oldest member of the House of Commons, and 'father' of the Liverpool City Council. He was born and bred in the midst of the people he represented. David Logan served the people of the Scotland Division giving splendid public service over a long period of years and was attentive to his duties till the end. Only a few weeks before he died, he attended a City Council meeting. His passing was mourned not only by his family and friends but also by people in many parts of the country, and particularly in his Scotland Road Constituency. 'The Universe and Catholic Times', February 28th, 1964, wrote:

> Alderman David Gilbert Logan, C.B.E., K.C.G., oldest Member of Parliament in British history, was a dedicated man. Dedicated of all to his Church and secondly to his fellow man. In the cause of both he was a dedicated fighter. Liverpool has lost a brilliant son, the people he represented are bereaved of a devoted father, and the poor are poorer still because an understanding friend has gone. He was the uncrowned King of the Scotland Division of Liverpool that he had represented since 1929. He held court in a humble home above a fish and chip shop in Kew Street, Scotland Road.

He had often been asked to live somewhere else. But it was in Scotland Road that he first realised the plight of the people around him. He represented them and it was right, he would say, that he should be there among them. Only extreme old-age compelled him to move to live with one of his daughters. David's wife, Mrs. Logan, whom he spent forty-three happy years, died in 1952.

He always attributed his understanding of human nature to his training as a pawnbroker. He once told a colleague in the Commons:

> Here we come into contact with many university men. My university days were spent behind a pawnshop counter, which would qualify anyone to speak of economic conditions and faults and foibles of human beings.

Joan Miller, David Logan's granddaughter tells her own story of her famous grandfather in this portrait:

> To his grandchildren, my grandfather was a very special man. Whenever we were in his company, he

would do his party piece-conjuring tricks, and then he would wait for our astonishment, with twinkling blue eyes. He had a dry sense of humour, and would keep his face straight, while saying something hilarious. I suppose it was the same when he mingled with other M. P.'s in the House of Commons, not letting others see his feelings. But if something upset him, he would be in fine fettle and have it thrashed out until he won.

If anyone needed help or advice, they only had to go to Dave Logan, and tell him of their problem, and he would take them to the appropriate authority and get it solved. No committee rooms for him – just his 'office' at the top of the stairs in his own house at 362 Scotland Road. This was his home until he was almost ninety years of age. He would not move from there, saying, "The people put me in Parliament, and they know where to find me here".

He hated poverty, discrimination and unfairness, and fought for the poor all his life. He never sought honours or fame, and turned down the chance to become Lord Mayor, and lived just for his constituents, fighting for decent housing and fair play in industry.

When he succeeded T. P. O'Connor in 1929, the people of Scotland Division walked alongside the car he was in through the streets to Lime Street Station. I sat on my mother's knee next to him. I wish I could remember that special time. The hopes of everyone were centred on him, and till he died, he never let them down.

Many years later, the people turned out, and I like the rest of my family followed his coffin. Women knelt with rosary beads in their hands everywhere along the route of the funeral, and policemen saluted as the hearse drove past. Everyone showed his or her feelings that day. A lot had been written about the oldest M. P., at the time, in the House of Commons, the Father of the House, and his lifetime of fighting for fair play in an unfair world, but to me he was just my "Granda".

20

John Hughes
Provision Merchant

John Hughes, born near Kilkeel Co. Down in 1866, entered Liverpool as a young man and worked in a general provision merchant's shop until he saved enough money to establish his own grocery business. This grew to be a huge enterprise comprising sixty retail grocery stores in and around Liverpool. His head office and wholesale department was at Derby Road, Bootle, about three miles down river from Liverpool City centre. He maintained strong links with Ireland and all things Irish. It was rumoured that seventy-five percent of his employees were Irish Catholics. They were encouraged to participate in Irish cultural events and to become involved with the firm's gaelic football team. Whenever possible, Irish produce was sold in his shops, much of it from Ballina, Co. Mayo. John Hughes made Limerick bacon and ham a speciality in his shops and helped to establish a reputation for these products in Britain.

In December 1898 there was great excitement in the Waterloo/Crosby area of Liverpool with the opening of new premises by John Hughes, as his shop in Church Road, Waterloo was no longer filling the needs of his customers. On the 24, December 1898 'The Herald' newspaper wrote:

> For some seven years past Mr Hughes has had a business establishment in Church Road, Waterloo as well as at 38 St. Johns Road. The former has long been entirely inadequate for the demand made upon its resources hence the removal into adjacent, but much larger, much more convenient and also much more commanding premises. Great interest filled the air as

people looked into the new shop. Thursday night being an object of great interest to numbers of spectators filled as it was with geese, fat turkeys and the provisions which one generally associates with the festive season and lit throughout by electric light. Four electric arc lights effect the outside illuminations, each of 1000w and as may be imagined the premises at night form a very conspicuous block in the main thoroughfare of Waterloo.

John Hughes had been in the provision trade for many years and occupied a position of being the largest retail seller in the district. His business motto would appear to be excellence in quality, associated with absolute moderation in price. He was noted for the excellent quality of his Irish goods, and was one of the largest importers of Irish bacon and hams together with Wiltshire bacon and Cumberland bacon and hams.

'The Herald' went on to praise John Hughes, for the excellent standard of eggs sold in his shops:

Of Irish eggs Mr. Hughes also makes a justly celebrated speciality. These may be relied upon as perfectly fresh, since they are collected daily by Mr. Hughes own buyers from the farmers and poultry keepers in Ireland.

The quality of the tea sold in John Hughes, shops also comes in for high praise.

Mr. Hughes' tea may also be safely styled delicious and pure, and moderate also in price. His 'Joy of Home' tea has been subjected to the severest of tests, and Mears, Norman Tate and Co., the well-known analyst, say, of it: "the result of our analyst of 'Joy of Home' tea indicates that it is a genuine tea, free from mixture with foreign or injurious substance. The liquid tea produced from it is strong of pleasant aroma and agreeable flavour.

Samples of the tea may be obtained free so that the public, without charge, may taste the quality claimed for it. The public, were also told that the sugars obtained in Mr. Hughes shops where obtained direct from the refiners, while the same lowness of price is also observed.'

By 1905 the premises at 62 South Road would no longer meet the requirements in floor space and the

134 South Road, Waterloo

business was relocated into much larger premises at 134, South Road, Waterloo. To alert the local population of the move a large advertisement was placed in 'The Herald' on Saturday, May 13th, 1905, which reads:

Hughes's new premises, 134, South Road Waterloo, opened Thursday, May 11th 1904. Owing to continued growth of his business in Waterloo, John Hughes has found it necessary to remove from 62, South Road to larger premises and more commodious premises which he opened with an entirely new stock of high class Teas, Groceries and Provisions. John Hughes regrets the many inconveniences and delays to which his customers have been subjected in the past owing to the inadequacy of the old premises, and begs to inform them and the public generally. That in the new premises there is ample accommodation for dealing efficiently with his extensive and increasing business, and for executing all orders with care and promptitude.

The provision department is stocked with a choice selection of the best brands of finest Irish, Danish and Canadian bacon and hams pale and smoked. Cheese finest prize dairy Cheshire, gorgonzola, stilton and Canadian cheese. Eggs large fresh Irish eggs, collected daily by his own buyers from the farmers in Ireland and equal in every way to new laid eggs. Butter the very choicest brands of Danish Kiel, Irish Creamery and Colonial butters. Hughes's butters are imported direct from the best dairies in Denmark, Ireland and the Colonies and are the finest the world produces, being perfect in colour and of delicious flavour. Orders by post or telephone (21 Waterloo) will receive the prompt and personal attention of the manager and will be despatched under his own supervision.

If the Waterloo store is an example of the care and detail paid to his customers, it is not hard to imagine why John Hughes' empire expanded to over sixty shops by the 1920's. The First World War had a big effect on John Hughes though he himself was not enlisted and he could not come to terms with the unnecessary loss of life among young men. In 1917 he returned home to live the rest of his life in Ireland, but still held onto his business interests in England.

On his return, John Hughes purchased a number of farms, among them the Westby Estate near Kiltegan, County Wicklow. John later offered part of the Westby Estate to the newly formed St. Patrick's Missionary Society. John also purchased an old house at Aghavannag, not far from the Kiltegan Estate. It was one of a string of army barracks built on the military road between Dublin and Glenmalure after the 1798 rebellion. The house had been a hunting lodge owned by Charles Stewart Parnell, whose home Avondale, was not far away and later, still the country home of John Redmond. John Hughes offered the house to St. Patrick's Missionary Society, but they turned it down. It later became a youth hostel run by 'An Oige'. In 1927 John Hughes sold his business of sixty shops to the Liverpool Co-operative Society.

He was a strong supporter of the nationalist cause. He made large contributions to the political party of 'Fianna Fail'. He was associated with the foundation of the 'Irish Press' newspaper, and was on its Board of Directors until his death, on March 12, 1934. The Irish press quoted Eamon de Valera as saying of him, "he was one of the grandest Irishmen I have ever meet."

21

Dr. Thomas McLaughlin

Most if not all of the portraits of people, in 'Liverpool's Irish Connection' have made a contribution to the City of Liverpool, however an exception is made with Thomas McLaughlin. The connection is not directly with Thomas but with his granddaughter, but his story is worth telling. Thomas's granddaughter Olwen McLaughlin runs a very successful Art Gallery in Cook Street in Liverpool City centre and has done so for many years. At times when we highlight outstanding people from the past we need the help of many wonderful people who have the interest of a city at heart. Olwen is one of those people, and very respected in the business community in the town.

When approached by Ron Formby, editor of the 'Scottie Press Community Newspaper' for help in promoting the name of William James Carling, who is also featured in this book, Olwen left no stone unturned to help, and the first exhibition of Carling's work took place in her gallery. It was during discussions in promoting Carling that the story of Thomas Mclaughlin came to the fore.

We live in an age of man's thirst for gas and oil, to enable us to drive our cars, light our homes and turn the wheels of industry. It was not always like that for most of the people of Ireland, at least not until people like Thomas McLaughlin came on the scene. In 1922 the birth of a nation was taking place and those who helped in its delivery came from every background of the Irish people. Many had a vision of what the nation would look like in the years that lay ahead and this is the story of one of those people.

Thomas was born in 1896 in Drogheda. He was educated by the Christian Brothers in Synge Street Dublin, and went on to attend University College Dublin. After completing the study of physics to Master's Degree, he became an engineer. He was then appointed to the staff of University College Galway to teach physics, and here he found time to complete a B.E. in electrical engineering. The following year he completed research into the behaviour of gas bubbles subjected to the action of an electrical field, and was awarded a Ph.D.

In 1922 Thomas McLaughlin armed himself with a slide-rule, a notebook and drawing paper. He had a dream that Ireland would one day compete with the rest of the world in a peaceful way, to bring prosperity to its people. He was concerned that the West of Ireland was without electricity, as it was only the larger towns or cities that had electrification schemes which were restricted, and very few houses had electric lighting. Thomas was a young man still in his early twenties and was working for the German Company, Seiman's, during this period.

During his time at University College Galway it was claimed that Frank Sharman Rishworth, Professor of Civil Engineering, was influential in his investigation of implementing a hydroelectric scheme on the Shannon.

Still in his early twenties, Thomas took himself off to London, determined to acquire practical experience in the British electrical industry, but without success. He was offered many jobs but one in the electrical industry eluded him. His determination eventually paid of, when he obtained a job with the German firm Siemans-Schuckett and he was sent to Berlin to study the design of power plants. He took the opportunity to visit power plants in operation and under construction. It was during this time that the idea of a hydro electrical scheme on the Shannon fermented in his mind, and he wrote:

No sincere student could have lived through that whole period of intense national enthusiasm without feeling a passionate desire to do all in his power to assist in national construction, and in the building up of the country by development from within. It was with this intense feeling I began my career abroad, and the ideal never for a moment left me until it brought me home again to see the Shannon Scheme realised. It was with little credit to me – I could know no mental peace, no sense of self-fulfilment until my mission in life, as it had then become to me, was realised. Everything I saw abroad, everything I read of, brought just one thought to my mind – can this development be applied at home? Could we have this in Ireland? Such were the natural yearnings of a youth of that inspiring period.

In Bavaria he saw a network similar to the one he wanted for the Shannon, an electricity scheme that extended like a spider's web all over the country, and he wrote:

To this area I went and studied for myself on the spot, always with the query in my mind – why not so in Ireland? I learned of the large-scale electricity networks of other countries, of Sweden and Switzerland, of Italy and France, of Canada and of the United States…. Quickly came the determination that at home in Ireland we must have a national network reaching to our cities, towns, villages and on to the rural areas. My country of which I was so intensely proud must not lag behind other lands.

It was Thomas McLaughlin who urged the government to set up its own Electricity Supply Board. In 1927 ESB was founded and Thomas was appointed as the first Managing Director. In 1929 the giant turbines of the Hydro Electrification Scheme came into operation at Ardnacrucha. The management and staff of ESB presented him with a silver replica scale model of the power plant of Ardnacrusha at the Gresham Hotel on the 6th May 1932. Thomas married Olwen O'Malley from Limerick, and the marriage produced three sons who were all successful in their own fields of law and architecture.

Thomas McLaughlin brought about much more than the electrification of Ireland with the Shannon Hydroelectric Scheme, he brought pride and determination to the people. He was twenty-six years of age, with nerves of steel when he presented himself in front of a government made up of men who had fought for Ireland's freedom. He convinced them that his Shannon Hydroelectric Scheme would be one of the greatest steps forward in Ireland's history. Perhaps one day a monument will be erected to this great man, a monument that will bring his name into every household in Ireland. On the 16 February 1971 the day after the death of Dr. Thomas Mclaughlin, P.P. O'Reilly paid the following tribute to Thomas on Radio Telefis Eireann:

The man who died in Spain yesterday has left Ireland the greatest physical memorial that any Irishman has given his country. For it was he who harnessed the Shannon and made it produce light and power. In 1923, working as a trainee engineer at the Siemens-Schuckert factory in Germany, the 26-year-old Tommy McLaughlin saw what Germany was doing harnessing electric power from the flow and fall of water and bringing this power on vast networks to every corner of the land. He asked himself why? Why not so in Ireland, where only one in every forty homes had electric light? He prepared his plans and returned at Christmas 1923 to a country dismayed and shattered by civil war; he cajoled the parties together, the reluctant government, and the hopeful German firm. When they needed money to do the preliminary surveys the Germans had none nor indeed the Government, he got it himself through a personal overdraft from a bank manager in Limerick. Then, backed by the government and particularly by the new Minister, Patrick McGilligan, the work began. Five thousand men created the great barriers of Ardnacrusha and Parteen, and our largest river was stopped in its course. 'It was Tommy McLaughlin who thought it all up,' said Doctor McGilligan.

On Wednesday, 27th August 2003 ESB celebrated its 75th birthday and family members of Thomas Mclaughlin attended the function. A time capsule with a number of historical documents was presented to the National Museum by Thomas McLaughlin's great grandson, Samuel Thomas on behalf of ESB.

22

Rose Anne Murphy

Rose Anne Murphy was born in Liverpool on the 11th February 1898, just a hundred years after the great rising in Ireland of 1798, a fact not lost on her during her lifetime. Rose Anne was the youngest of thirteen children. Her parents came to Liverpool from Dundalk. James Murphy had worked for John Jameson, the whiskey merchant, before they came to Liverpool. He and his wife Mary Eliza Carroll, were also born in Dundalk Ireland. The first child of that union in Mulingar, Ireland was Mary Kate Murphy, One child was born in France and the remainder in England. All of the Murphy children spent much of their childhood in their Irish homeland.

Though born in Liverpool, Rose Anne Murphy spent a great deal of her childhood in Dundalk. There were in those days frequent ferryboats between Liverpool and Dundalk and so Rose Anne never had any doubts as to where her loyalties lay. In 1915 Rose Anne joined 'Cumann Na mBann', which was the female arm of a newly formed branch which had been formed in Liverpool. She was also a member of the Gaelic League and a local Camogie team, which played in Sefton Park. Annie Gerrity, a lifelong friend of Rose, said she was reputed to be able to hit a ball as good as any man and Rose later became the captain of the team. Nora Thornton was the leader of the Liverpool Cumann Na mBann. Her brother Frank Thornton was the leader of the Volunteers in Liverpool, and he later became a T.D. in Ireland. Her son commenting on his mother's involvement in the Irish struggle for freedom wrote:

On the first of August 1915 the funeral of the great Fenian O'Donaven Rosa took place at Glasnevin Cemetery Dublin. This is, were Padraic Pearse (President of the Provisional Government 1916) gave his famous oration about the Fenian dead. Rose Anne and other members of Liverpool Cumann Na mBann took part in the funeral commemorations, the funeral souvenir brochure, a historic document in its own right she kept all her life, eventually passing it on the her son. Back in Liverpool the First World War was going badly as there where not enough volunteers to fight and so conscription was introduced. One of Rose Anne's brothers went to the U.S.A. and did not return for twenty years.

Rose Anne continued her training with the Cumann Na mBann in Duke Street Liverpool. This, included first aid, the taking of messages, intelligence work and also rifle shooting we knew this from her own account. She always remained a very good marksman. The Irish Volunteers also trained in rifle shooting in a cellar of a Duke Street house.

At Easter 1916, six women left Liverpool, crossing over to Dublin on the night of Holy Thursday to attend a Cumann Na mBann training camp in the Dublin Mountains. They were Rose Ann Murphy, Peggy and Frances Downey, Anastasia MacLouglin, Kathleen Murphy and Kathy Dornan. On reaching

Dublin they met up with their leader Nora Thornton, who had crossed over a few days earlier to arrange the camp, to which they were then taken. The rising was planned to take place on Easter Sunday but was cancelled on the order of Eoin Mac Niell, leader of the volunteers. The Liverpool contingent of the Cumann Na mBann were instructed to attend a ceildh in Fredrick Street, which they duly did. That night they were all locked in the dance hall until the following morning. Rose Anne thought that it might well have been Michael Collins who locked them in.

The next day the 24th of April 1916 they were ordered to report to the G.P.O. (General Post Office) in O'Connell Street where they were all given various tasks to perform. Captain Turner had been assigned to the defence of Hopkins and Hopkins, a shop on the corner of O'Connell Street and Eden Quay. He asked for volunteers to help him transport supplies across O'Connell Street. Rose Anne Murphy volunteered for this task. Captain Turner recorded this in his report on the 5th June 1926 and thanked a young Liverpool girl for her help. Rose Anne was that girl, she was just turned 18 years. After helping Captain Turner, she returned to the G.P.O. It may have been on the Tuesday 25th of April that Rose Anne was told to take a message down to Dundalk and try to get the volunteers there to rise, and explain to them what the situation was like in Dublin.

Rose Anne made her way from the G.P.O. to Amiens Street Railway Station (now called Connolly Street Station) and there boarded a train for Dundalk. However a bridge had been blown between Lusk and Rush so Rose Anne got off the train and proceeded to walk the remaining forty miles to Dundalk.

On arrival, Rose Anne sort out the Captain of the volunteers, who happened to be her cousin, Vincent Hughes. Later after the surrender of the volunteers in Dublin Rose Anne made her way back to Liverpool and, as they say, lived to fight another day.

W.J. Brennan Whitmore in his book, 'With The Irish in Frongoch', wrote:

1,863 men were sent to Frongoch Prison Camp in Bala North Wales, one of those prisoners was a particular friend of Rose Anne and during his time in the prison camp made her a Cumann Na mBann brooch in the shape of a rifle with the name of Cumann Na mBann interwoven into it. This was the only recognition of Rose Anne's part in the rising although she applied for her 1916 medal it met with a negative response from the government of the day.

It would appear that women in the Ireland of thirty years ago were still very much second-class citizens. Rose Anne was also, in my opinion, entitled to the War of Independence Medal as she and other members of Cumann Na mBann were active in Liverpool, fighting for Irish independence. It is not generally known that Liverpool had the largest active group of volunteers outside of Ireland. At that time Michael Collins had visited Liverpool and Liam Mellows who was in charge of supplies and armaments was a more frequent visitor.

Bernard Morgan said of his mother, the man who I suspect of making Rose Anne's Cumann Na mBann brooch in Frongoch, was Neil Kerr who was accidentally shot in 1920 while awaiting a supply of arms from Liam Mellows. But then Liverpool's fight and contribution to Irish Freedom has not yet been fully told. In 1929 Rose Anne Murphy married a Dundalk man, named Henry Joseph Morgan.

Rose Anne died at the age of eighty-four in 1984 in Warrington General Hospital. She was buried at Runcorn, Cheshire. Tom Walsh of the Liverpool Irish Centre spoke at the funeral and recalled her lifelong commitment to Ireland. Frank Dolan's weekly column, in the 'Irish Post', commenting on Rose Anne Murphy, stated:

Although a great age, she was active right up to a few weeks before her death and a regular visitor at Liverpool's Irish Centre. Each Sunday afternoon for many years Liverpool's veterans of the Rising and of the War of independence used to meet at the Centre. By the late Seventies, however, their numbers had dwindled to such an extent that the meetings ceased.

Frank Dolan, went on to recall the recent death of Mrs Peggy Viant, nee Downey. At the weekend in Sudbury-on-Thames, Surrey. She would have been 87 in August and she was Peggy Downey, born in Liverpool and another of that gallant band. She and her sister crossed to Dublin on the Holy Thursday night and, like Rose Morgan were in the G.P.O. It seems most likely that, with the deaths of Mrs. Morgan and Mrs. Viant, the last of Britain's 1916 Rising participants have gone.

During the First World War thirty-eight men of the Royal Flying Corps, top fighter 'aces' were Irish. They were Standish Conn O'Grady, Paddy Langan Byrne, Joe Callaghan, Eddie Hariten and Patrick Cockren. The top ace of the Royal Flying Corps is credited with destroying seventy-three enemy aircraft. He was Major Edward Mick Mannock, who was killed in action near Lillers, France, on 26th July 1918. At 31 years of age he was the recipient of the Victoria Cross, (V.C.) Distinguished Service Order (D.S.O.) and the Military Cross (M.C.). Rose Anne Murphy was a young woman living in Liverpool during the First World War and like her fellow countrymen she too was brave and fought for the freedoms she believed in, at a time when Ireland was demanding its independence.

The Liverpool Irish have fought gallantly for the United Kingdom in many wars. Many of the Irish regiments in the British Army would have included the Liverpool Irish in their ranks. The right to freedom and justice would have been born in those men. Would this, have been the reason, that some of their sons and daughters fought for Ireland's freedom in later years? In the case of Rose Anne Murphy, she paid the price with the loss of her husband Henry Joseph Morgan, in the Second World War as he died defending freedom while serving in the Merchant Service.

23

Serving Scotland and Vauxhall Wards

James Whitty, born in County Wexford in 1813, was a cousin of Michael James Whitty (chapter 5). In 1848, James set himself up in business as a woollen draper in Liverpool and after securing his company, he turned his attention to the terrible poverty in the town. This soon drew him into politics, he joined the 'Liberal Party'. He became a councillor for the 'Vauxhall Ward', 1863-73. Later he became a member of the school board and a magistrate. He was also the first Catholic to serve on the 'Select Vestry', between 1853-65.

Following his death, aged 63 years in 1876, a Requiem Mass took place at the Catholic Pro-Cathedral on Copperas Hill and such was the popularity of the man that people of all shades of political and religious belief attended his funeral. Many notable people in the Irish community were present including Dr. John Bligh and Dr. Alexander Murray Bligh and Charles Corbally, nephew of Alderman Richard Shiel. After the Mass the cortege made its way along London Road, Norton Street, St. Anne Street, Cazneau Street, Scotland Road and Stanley Road before arriving at Ford Cemetery.

George Jeremy Lynskey, was born in Ashgrove, Tuam, Galway in September 1861 and was one of fourteen children. The legal profession in Liverpool was to benefit as he worked in the practice of W. Madden, a fellow Irishman, (O'Hare, Lynskey, Flynn, Madden) before setting up his own practice – Lynskey Solicitors, 30 Lord Street, his home address being, 2 Seymour Road, Broad Green Liverpool. He was an Alderman on the Liverpool council and a prominent Irish Nationalist.

Charles Stewart Parnell, leader of the Irish Parliamentary Party, chose Lynskey as legal adviser during the memorial parliamentary election in the Irish National League of Great Britain and he filled this advisory role for many years. During the Dock Strike of 1887 he was one of the leading members of the Irish community together with Patrick Byrne, and he and others tried to bring relief to the dockers' families. In 1890, Lynskey was one of the mourners at the funeral of Patrick Byrne.

In 1889 he was returned to the Liverpool City Council for Scotland Ward. He continued to represent this ward until 1895, when under the City Extension Scheme, it was sub-divided. As a candidate for South Scotland Ward Lynskey again succeeded by a large majority along with his brother in-law Mr Patrick Kearney who had four sons and two daughters and died on 28th October 1921.

Lynskey's eldest son, Sir George Justin Lynskey, was born in Knotty Ash, Liverpool on 5th February 1888. He joined his father's firm and was called to the Bar in 1920. He married Eileen Prendiville, from Liverpool, in 1913, and they lived at 12 Queens Way, Liverpool. He died December 1957 aged sixty-nine. The 'Sunday Pictorial', December 12th, 1948 stated:

> Like plenty of Irishmen, Lynskey was born in Liverpool. But as an Irishman he will tell you, that doesn't make him English. George Lynskey became a prominent member of the Bar on the Northern Circuit. One of the pupils in his chambers was Sir David Maxwell Fyfe. On Lynskey's advice, he also "went north" to launch a brilliant career. In 1930, Lynskey took silk and became a K.C. in 1937.
>
> The Lyskey's entertain little, and seldom go out in the evenings. When the day's work is done, the judge still finds plenty to do at home. But he doesn't let it interfere with his listening to his fellow Liverpudlian Tommy Handley in Itma. He has a taste for dance music, in the summer, when he is not sitting, he can usually be found at Lord's for he is a great cricket

lover, and since his residence is in the south, he has transferred his allegiance to Middlesex – with reservations when they play Lancashire. He is also a football fan - his team is Everton.

Another member of the council was Alderman T. G. Taggart born in Quarter Grange County Tyrone in 1861. He was elected to represent Vauxhall Ward in 1888 and was employed by Tate and Lyle (sugar refinery), a man of sober habits a non-drinker or smoker, and lived at St. Domingo Grove, Everton.

He was the first unequivocally working-class member of the Council. Until 1905 all the six working-class members on the Council were Irish Nationalists (including Trade Union and Co-operative Society Officials) who were members of the Labour Party. Taggart voiced strong opposition in the Council to the demolition policy on behalf of the inhabitants of the slums. It meant that people were thrown onto the street without alternative accommodation. The Tories who were in a majority on the Council, kept hold of committee chairmanships and only the least important would be given over to the opposition. Alderman Taggart was chairman of the Burials Committee in 1914. He died on the 12 April 1920 aged 61. 'The Daily Post' of Monday April 13 1920, stated:

In Alderman Taggart the City Council loses one of its ablest debaters as well as one of its oldest members, for the late Alderman's record of thirty-eight years of continuous service is only excelled by Sir William Forwood and Alderman Fredrick Smith. A staunch Irish Nationalist in politics in his younger days he was an ardent and at times aggressive advocate of his country's aspirations and in this capacity figured in many a heated scene in the Council Chamber, but under the mellowing influence of time he and his opponents got to know each other better.

John Patrick Kelly was another Irish nationalist to receive an aldermanic seat, born, in Moy County Tyrone 1869 and was one of eleven children. In November 1925 he became an alderman with Liverpool City Council, Liverpool Daily Post printed:

Politically Mr. Kelly was an uncompromising Irish Home Ruler. For twenty-years, he acted as honorary secretary of the Liverpool branch of the United Irish League and in this capacity organised many demonstrations and banquets. During later crises in Ireland he was an active Sinn Feinner and became president of the Irish Self Determination League. At one time he was marked down for internment and evaded arrest for some time, but was placed under arrest in Wormwood Scrubs at the time of an Irish demonstration in London in June 1921. Shortly after a truce was arranged and Mr. Kelly was released on the direct intervention of Mr. Lloyd George. The Irish treaty, which followed, did not fully please him.

The founding of the 'Irish Club', Kirkdale, which was founded in 1899 at 142 Stanley Road, Kirkdale, Liverpool gave great service to the Irish community. J. M. McElroy served as Hon. Secretary. The club was very much a community-based organisation that reached out to the wider community. The people of the Scotland Road and Vauxhall area certainly played a big part in the activities of the Irish Club. On the 19th September 1915, the Ancient Order of Hibernians held a meeting at St. Martins Hall, Scotland Road. The main reason for the meeting was to raise awareness of the need to find funds for Catholic schools, temperance and a Catholic press. The main speaker was Bro. J. Nugent, M.P. and a section of Irish songs and music was given by the Hibernian Concert Party, the printing of the programmes by T. Kilburn 209 Scotland Road.

In 1916 the club undertook to set up, 'Liverpool Irish Committee' a fund to provide comforts for the 8th Irish at the front, and those imprisoned in Germany.

On Friday, November 30th, 1917, a Ladies' Bohemian Concert took place, in Exchange Station Hotel, Liverpool. This was in aid of funds to provide comforts for the 8th Irish at the front.

Another group of people who served the Vauxhall area were survivors of the famine in Ireland. Jim Fitzsimons had turned eighty years of age when he took on the task of writing the story of Saint Augustine's Church, which stood on Great Howard Street. Jim was passionate in the opening lines of his story:

> It seems so sad with the nearing of the 21st century that a more close and intimate recording of people's origins, endeavours and experiences has not been documented. How they lifted up their lives from abject poverty and obscurity from the mid-19th century.

Jim's story is about his neighbours and that of his own family, who arrived in Liverpool with only the skills of those who lived by the land. The farming skills that had been passed down over many generations in Ireland were of little use in a growing seaport. They came in the tens of thousands to escape the famine of 1845 to 1849 only to inhabit the worst type of housing. Jim based his story around Saint Augustine's Church that stood on Great Howard Street, about a mile down river from the Pier Head.

The people in the community that served Saint Augustine's moved into better housing some distance away from the church and it was crushed by the power of the bulldozer. Jim makes it clear from the beginning of his memoir how proud he was of the people of Saint Augustine's, because ninety-five percent of the community were from Ireland, he wrote:

> It is inevitable because of the circumstances during the mid-nineteenth century that the people of Ireland

are mainly involved in this history. But this is inescapable as almost ninety-five percent of the population of this small area of the Saint Augustine parish originally came from that country. Prior to formation of the Parish of St. Augustine the history of the area is necessary for the reader to know and try to understand the kind of life the Irish immigrant from the middle and latter part of the nineteenth century both physically and mentally. He concludes by blaming successive British governments for giving too little help the reason for the huge immigration from Ireland was basically political with little help for people during the famine years to the detriment of the Irish nation by successive British Governments.

Jim describes Liverpool as a stepping-stone to a better life across the seas, but for many of them that dream never materialised. Although many just about had enough money to sail on to America, they would be deceived or robbed by the conmen of the town while waiting for a ship to cross the ocean. It would be the descendants of those who stayed in Liverpool, whether by choice or unavoidable circumstances who would realise the dreams of their forefathers.

Jim's story is about his people, the Irish and how they and their priests living in poverty built their school and church of Saint Augustine, so that further generations of the Liverpool Irish would have a better future. Sixteen thousand people lived in this small area and many died on the streets from hunger and fever caused by the overcrowded hovels, in what would become the parish of Saint Augustine. Jim tells his readers of the formation of the Parish of St. Augustine:

It was at a meeting of parishioners in St Mary's, Highfied Street School on the 12th October 1848. The subject was to raise a memorial to the memory of the Benedictine monks who died of typhoid fever in 1847 helping the people who had fallen ill. At further meetings held in a warehouse at the corner of Chadwick Street and Great Howard Street it was decided to erect a church to the late lamented priests of St. Mary's. As a tribute to the monks who died in the fever of 1849, the church of St. Augustine was opened on the 9th September 1848 as a Chapel of Ease and sometimes entitled, the 'Martyr's Church'.

The Kirkdale Irish Club, was founded in 1899 at 142 Stanley Road, Kirkdale Liverpool. J. M. McElroy served as Hon. Secretary. The club was very much a community based organisation that reached out to the wider Irish community. The people of the Scotland Road and Vauxhall area certainly played a big part in the activities of the Irish Club. On the 15th December 1915, the Ancient order of Hibernians held a meeting at St. Martin's Hall, Scotland Road.

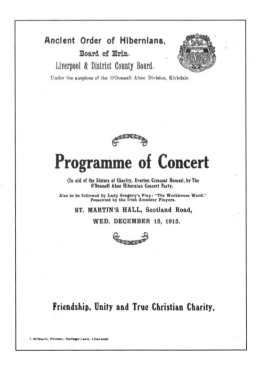

The main reason for the meeting was to raise awareness of the need to find funds for Catholic schools, temperance and a Catholic press. The main speaker was Bro. J. Nugent, M.P. and a section of Irish songs and music was given by the Hibernian Concert Party the programmes printed by T. Kilburn 209 Scotland Road.

In 1916 the club undertook to set up 'Liverpool Irish Committee' a fund to provide comforts for the 8th Irish at the front, and those imprisoned in Germany. On Friday, November 30th, 1917, a Ladies' Bohemian Concert took place, in Exchange Station Hotel, Liverpool. This was in aid of funds to provide comforts for the 8th Irish at the front.

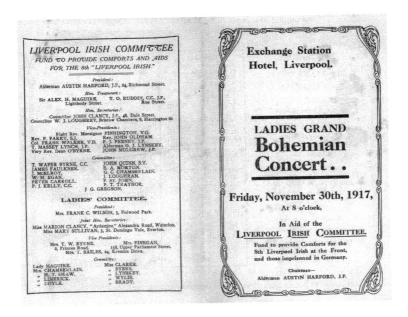

Committee members of Liverpool Irish Club, Kirkdale
John McEvoy, Hon Secretary, fourth from, left front row.

1920 unveiling of Celtic Cross to the Liverpool Irish
who fell in 1914-18 War.

1920 Communion at Holy Cross, Sunday Morning,
day after unveiling of Celtic Cross.

Bibliography

Bligh, John & Alexander Murray
Liverpool's Legion of Honour 1893
Liverpool Medical Institution Transactions 1968
British Medical Journal March 1968
Munk's Roll (Vol V1, p. 51)

Byrne, John
Post and Mercury, Death of John Byrne. 27 November 1915
Liverpool Review, September 1903

Byrne, Patrick
Enniscorthy Guardian, Liverpool Memorial Honours Ferns Man.   24
    July 1961
Liberal Review, The Fight on the First. 25 October 1879
Liverpool Review, In the City Council. 7 April 1888
The Liverpool Citizen, The Police and the Orange Riot. 3 July 1889
Liverpool Citizen, Men in Danger. 11 September 1889
Liverpool Courier, Death of Mr. P. Byrne. 5, 6, May 1890
Liverpool Daily Post, Vauxhall Ward. 3 November 1884
Liverpool Daily Post, Death of Mr. Councillor Byrne, May 1890
Liverpool Mercury, The Late Mr. Councillor Byrne 6, 8, May 1890
Liberal Review, Jottings of the Week. 3 December 1881
Liberal Review The Elections 19, November 1881
Liberal Review, Jottings of the Week. 4 November 1882
Liverpool Review, Pat and the Spoons. 5 June 1887
Liverpool Review, An Irish Forth Party. 11 July 1885
Liverpool Review, Jottings of the Week. 14 November 1885
Liverpool Review, Dandy Pat's Mess of Pottage. 5 November 1887
Liverpool Review, Dandy Pat Tells About Liverpool Scavengers.
    14 September 1889
Liverpool Review, St. Patrick's Day in Liverpool 15 March 1890
Liverpool Review, What Pat Byrne Should Say. 14 January 1888
Liverpool Review, News In A Nutshell. 21 January 1888
Liverpool Review, Liverpool and Dublin 4 February 1888
Liverpool Review, Dandy Pat. 3 May, 1890
Liverpool Review, Ireland. 1, April 1885
Liverpool Review, The Byrne Memorial. 24 May 1890

Carling, James
James Carling Illustrations of Edgar Allen Poe's The Raven, edited by
    Roscoe Brown Fisher

Fitzsimons, Jim
Saint Augustines, Great Howard Street, Liverpool. A brief history by Jim Fitzsimons, published by Starfish Multimedia

Jones, Agnes
A Gifted Touch by James Cosbie Ross and John Ross published 1988
Liverpool Catholic Home Almanac for 1906
Memorials of Agnes Elizabeth Jones by her Sister 1871 published by Strahan & Co
Northern Ireland Hospitals North-West Management Committtee. 6 April 1954
Sydney Jones Library, Liverpool University Memorials of Agnes Elizabeth Jones

Murphy, Rose Ann
Ruth Taillon, 'When History Was Made – The Women of 1916', published by Beyond The Pale Publications 1996
Frank Dolan's Weekly Comment, Irish Post, May 22, 1982
'Irish democrat' October/November 2002, Peter Berresford Ellis, Column Mick Mannock, fighter pilot and curious socialist

Muspratt, James
My Life My Work by Edmund Knowles Muspratt

O'Connor, T. P.
Catholic Family Annual and Almanac for the Diocese of Liverpool 1888
Liverpool Review, A Man of The Week 23 March 1896
Liverpool Review, Recent Events 17th to 23 March 1896
Liverpool Review, page 6, April 12 1890
Liverpool's Legion of Honour, by B. Guinness Orchard 1893
Memoirs of an old Parliamentarian by T. P. O'Connor, M. P. 1899
T. P. O'Connor and The Liverpool Irish, L. W. Brady 1983
The Irish In Britain from The Earliest Times to the Fall and Death of Parnell, John Denvir 1892
Liverpool's Legion of Honour 1893
Liverpool Daily Post 11, June 1955

Shiel, Richard Alderman
Catholic Family Annual and Almanac for the Diocese of Liverpool 1888
Porcupine, Pen Portraits of Town Councillors. 9 September 1865
Porcupine, Death of Alderman Richard Shiel 4, March 1871
Memorials of Liverpool Vol. 2, by J. A. Picton, F.S.A. 1875
Liverpool's Legion of Honour by B. Guinness Orchard, published by the author at 72 Bridge Street, Birkenhead in 1893
The Porcupine pp 355
A History of the Corporation of Liverpool 1835-1914 by Brian D. White

Whitty, Michael James
Memorials of Liverpool Vol. 1, by J. A. Picton, F.S.A. 1875
Porcupine, Michael James Whitty 7 September 1872
Michael James Whitty, Tales of Irish Life, 2 vols. (1822-1824) Illustrated by his friend George Cruikshank. Later translated into French and German in 1826
Oxford University Press 1995

Whitty, May, Dame
Dame of the Theatre by Eric Johns, Arlington House, New York 1974
The Same Only Different by Margaret Webster London, Victor Gollancz Ltd 1969

Appendix

Bligh, John

Dr. John Bligh lived at 109 Mount Pleasant. His son Dr. John Patrick Bligh had a practice at 138 Fountains Road, Kirkdale, Liverpool.

Byrne, Patrick

Councillor Pat De Lacy Garton was an Irish fish merchant in Liverpool, who helped in the escape of James Stephens, the Fenian Leader from prison in Dublin. Stephens was taken from Ireland in a fish hooker owned by Pat De Lacy Garton.

Cruickshank, George

Cruickshank also illustrated for Goldsmith, Defoe, Scott, Dickens, to name a few.

Johnson, Joan

Born 7th November 1915, died at East Grinstead, Sussex, 8th October 2000: bringing an end to direct contact with Robert Noonan.

Jones, Agnes

Memorials of Agnes Elizabeth Jones by her Sister:

Liverpool workhouse. "In the present day of active benevolence and prompt investigation of wrong, all classes of the poor, oppressed and sinful, seem to be brought under the eye of the public. And assistance, solace and (as far as maybe) remedy, are provided; not, indeed, in any degree equal to the demand, for as riches increase and luxuries become more and more necessaries of life, so in proportion does poverty increase and wretchedness and woe superabound. Of all misery in the mass, however, no department was so long overlooked as the misery of work-house paupers".

Leblance, Nicholas

Nicholas Leblance born 1742-1806, chemist, in 1775. His attention was attracted by the offer of a prize by the French academy for a method of making soda from salt.

Muspratt, Edmund Knowles

Member of Liverpool Town Council, 1877-1886.
Member of Lancashire Council, 1889-1902.

Muspratt, James

Chemical processes have created pesticides and fertilisers for farmers, pharmaceuticals for the health care, industry, synthetic dyes and fibres for the textile industry. Pioneers like Muspratt brought into being beauty aids for the cosmetics industry, soap, synthetic sweeteners and flavours for the food industry, plastics for the packaging industry, chemicals and artificial rubber for the auto industry.

Chemical industries can be traced back to Middle Eastern artisans, who refined alkali and limestone for the production of glass as early as 7,000 B.C., to the Phoenicians who produced soap in the 6th century B.C., and to the Chinese who developed black powder, a primitive explosive around the 10th century. A.D. In the Middle Ages, alchemists produced small amounts of chemicals and by 1635 the Pilgrims in Massachusetts were producing saltpeter for gunpowder and chemicals for tanning. In the 1890s, German companies began mass producing sulphuric acid and at about the same time, chemical companies began using the electrolytic method, which required large amounts of electricity and salt, to create caustic soda and chlorine.

Man-made fibres changed the textile industry when rayon (made from wood fibres) was introduced in 1914. The introduction of synthetic fertilisers by the American Cyanamid Company in 1909 led to a green revolution in agriculture that dramatically improved crop yields. Advances in the manufacture of plastics led to the invention of celluloid in 1869 and the creation of such products as nylon by Du Pont in 1928. Research in organic chemistry in the 1910s allowed companies in the 1920s and 30s to begin producing chemicals from petrochemicals made from oil which became the industry's largest sector. Synthetic rubber came into existence during World War II, when the war cut off supplies of rubber from Asia.

James Muspratt died in Liverpool, May 4 1886. A large mill belonging to Kelloggs now stands on the site of Seaforth Hall and at the back of it is the Gladstone Dock. The pioneering work of James Muspratt, was carried on by his grandson, Sir Max Muspratt, who was Chairman of United Alkali Co Ltd and in 1924 became a director of the giant ICI Company.

O'Connor, T. P.

In 1873 the Home Rule Confederation of great Britain was formed, and Isaac Butt was elected president and was succeeded by Charles Stewart Parnell in 1877. T. P. O'Connor was proposed by Parnell and elected to the Presidency in 1883.

O'Connor was also elected for the Irish constituency of Galway Borough but he relinquished this seat. He continued to be unopposed during elections,

1918   1922   1923   1924   1929

Shiel, Richard Henry

National Library of Ireland.
Letter book of Richard Henry Sheil 1850-1856.
Subjects

1) Irish-England-Liverpool-19th century
2) Merchants-England-Liverpool-19th century
3) Lumber trade-Cuba-19th century
4) Lumber trade-England-Liverpool-19th century
5) Cuba-Description and travel-19th century
6) Liverpool (England)-commerce-Cuba-19th century
7) Cuba-Commerce-England-Liverpool-19 century
8) Some letters from Richard Henry Sheil, in French and Spanish.

Whitty, Alfred

Alfred was to be heir to his father's 'Daily Post', and was to pass it on, in turn, to his son. However, Michael James Whitty was not too happy with Alfred's life style and his recklessness in business so the 'Daily Post' was sold outright to Edward Russell who was then its first editor. Michael felt he had chosen a great editor, who was to become the future Lord Russell of Liverpool.

Whitty, Dame, May

Some of her films,
> Night Must Fall
> The Lady Vanishes
> 1939 Conquest
> 1940 Raffles, Bill of Divorcement
> 1941 Suspicion
> 1943 For Ever and a Day,
> The Constant Nymph,
> Lassie Come Home,
> Flesh and Fantasy,
> Madam Currie.
> The White Cliffs of Dover,
> Gas Light.
> My Name is Julia Ross.
> Devotion.
> Green Dolphin Street.
> If Winter Comes,
> The Return of October.

Personal quotes from Dame May Whitty.
"I've got everything Betty Grable has – only I've had it longer".

Whitty, Michael James

The 'Liverpool Catholic Home Almanac' for 1906, recorded the riots of 1835:

In 1835 the Irish quarter of Liverpool extended from Dale Street to Park Lane. Town improvements drove a wedge through the district and formed north and south colonies of Irish. As far back as that year Orange and Green riots took place in Liverpool, and the July meeting of 1835 led to a fierce fight in Park Lane, those arrested being forcibly released by the Irish from the Vauxhall Bridewell.

Robert Emmet (1778-1803) expelled from Trinity Collage, Dublin for his suspected support of the insurrection of 1798. He travelled to France in August 1800 to try and enlist French military aid. He returned to Ireland in 1802 convinced France would soon invade England, which he thought would give Ireland her opportunity to break free from England. Robert Emmet died on September 20, 1803.